Rethinking
HOMEWORK

Best Practices That Support Diverse Needs

ASCD MEMBER BOOK

Many ASCD members received this book as a
member benefit upon its initial release.

Learn more at: **www.ascd.org/memberbooks**

SUSTAINABLE
FORESTRY
INITIATIVE

Certified Fiber Sourcing

www.sfiprogram.org

ASCD cares about Planet Earth.
This book has been printed on environmentally friendly paper.

Rethinking HOMEWORK

Best Practices That Support Diverse Needs

by CATHY VATTEROTT

ASCD | Alexandria, Virginia USA

ASCD®

1703 N. Beauregard St. • Alexandria, VA 22311-1714 USA
Phone: 800-933-2723 or 703-578-9600 • Fax: 703-575-5400
Web site: www.ascd.org • E-mail: member@ascd.org
Author guidelines: www.ascd.org/write

Gene R. Carter, *Executive Director;* Nancy Modrak, *Publisher;* Scott Willis, *Director,
Book Acquisitions & Development;* Julie Houtz, *Director of Book Editing & Production;*
Miriam Goldstein, *Editor;* Greer Wymond, *Senior Graphic Designer;* Mike Kalyan,
Production Manager; Circle Graphics, *Typesetter*

All Web links in this book are correct as of the publication date below but may
have become inactive or otherwise modified since that time. If you notice a
deactivated or changed link, please e-mail books@ascd.org with the words "Link
Update" in the subject line. In your message, please specify the Web link, the book
title, and the page number on which the link appears.

ASCD Member Book, No. FY09-8 (July 2009, PS). ASCD Member Books mail to Pre-
mium (P) and Select (S) members on this schedule: Jan., PS; Feb., P; Apr., PS; May, P;
July, PS; Aug., P; Sept., PS; Nov., PS; Dec., P. Select membership was formerly known
as Comprehensive membership.

PAPERBACK ISBN: 978-1-4166-0825-7   ASCD product #108071

Also available as an e-book through ebrary, netLibrary, and many online booksellers
(see Books in Print for the ISBNs).

Quantity discounts for the paperback edition only: 10–49 copies, 10%; 50+ copies,
15%; for 1,000 or more copies, call 800-933-2723, ext. 5634, or 703-575-5634. For desk
copies: member@ascd.org.

Library of Congress Cataloging-in-Publication Data
Vatterott, Cathy, 1951-
  Rethinking homework : best practices that support diverse needs / Cathy Vatterott.
    p. cm.
  Includes bibliographical references and index.
  ISBN 978-1-4166-0825-7 (pbk. : alk. paper) 1. Homework. 2. Motivation in education.
I. Title.
  LB1048.V37 2009
  371.3'0281–dc22
                                                                        2009010371

18 17 16 15 14 13 12 11 10 09 1 2 3 4 5 6 7 8 9 10 11 12

For the children—

May their backpacks be light and their learning joyful.

Rethinking HOMEWORK

Best Practices That Support Diverse Needs

• • •

Acknowledgments

My thanks go first to ASCD for an educational vision that has guided my career and for the forum it has provided for my ideas. I am honored to be an ASCD author. I also wish to thank Debbie Howerton and Ann Cunningham-Morris, who doggedly encouraged me to put pen to paper, and especially Scott Willis, who served as my editor, cheerleader, and taskmaster, and who smoothed the rough edges from some of my most passionate rants. Thanks also to Miriam Goldstein for her thoughtful suggestions and her meticulous attention to detail.

My special thanks go to five authors who started and refined the conversation about homework and helped to guide my work.

The first of these authors are Etta Kralovec and John Buell, whose groundbreaking book *The End of Homework: How Homework Disrupts Families, Overburdens Children, and Limits Learning* (2000) dared to question an entrenched practice and first gave me comfort that I was not alone in my concerns.

Next, thanks to Alfie Kohn, whose numerous writings and presentations have greatly influenced my work. More than any other author, Alfie challenged me to think outside the box, to question the status quo, and to be irreverent without apology. On a personal note, his question to me—"What book do you want to write?"—was the homework *I* needed to do to shape the direction of this book. His book *The Homework Myth: Why Our Kids Get Too Much of a Bad Thing* (2006) critiqued the beliefs and norms about homework that we take for granted and proved to be great inspiration for my ideas.

I also owe thanks to Sara Bennett and Nancy Kalish, whose book *The Case Against Homework: How Homework Is Hurting Our Children and What We Can Do About It* (2006) poignantly shared the homework dilemmas of families and galvanized a parental movement for reasonable homework. Their book gave voice and dignity to the parent's perspective and legitimized the right of parents to be part of the homework discussion. Etta, Alfie, and Sara were never too busy to talk to me and to share their thoughts and resources. Their support was unyielding and their insights invaluable in the shaping of my ideas. I thank them for validating my "crusade" to reform homework practices.

This book would not be the same without the questions, insights, and examples provided by hundreds of teachers, administrators, and parents who attended my workshops and institutes over the last 10 years. Their questions challenged my ideas, their reflections caused me to rethink, and the examples they shared from their classrooms and schools made it all real. Especially important were the teachers and administrators whose thoughts and practices are featured in this book.

Many other people contributed to this book. I had numerous conversations with friends, families, and other parents (sometimes strangers on a plane), all anxious to share their opinions and personal stories about homework. I have never tired of those discussions—it's been great fun. Thanks also to my husband Glenn, who patiently endured long conversations about homework at parties, family gatherings, and social events, never once trying to change the subject.

And finally, to my son Andrew, who started it all. His learning struggles in elementary school frustrated me as both a parent and an educator and were the driving force that first caused me to question the value of homework. Thanks to the dedication, creativity, and perseverance of his special education teachers, he survived and eventually thrived as a student. Watching Andrew grow into a successful college student has been one of the greatest joys and affirmations of my life. I wrote this book for other students like him.

1

The Cult(ure) of Homework

Homework is a long-standing education tradition that, until recently, has seldom been questioned. The concept of homework has become so ingrained in U.S. culture that the word *homework* is part of the common vernacular, as exemplified by statements such as these: "Do your homework before taking a trip," "It's obvious they didn't do their homework before they presented their proposal," or "The marriage counselor gave us homework to do." Homework began generations ago when schooling consisted primarily of reading, writing, and arithmetic, and rote learning dominated. Simple tasks of memorization and practice were easy for children to do at home, and the belief was that such mental exercise disciplined the mind. Homework has generally been viewed as a positive practice and accepted without question as part of the student routine. But over the years, homework in U.S. schools has evolved from the once simple tasks of memorizing math facts or writing spelling words to complex projects.

As the culture has changed, and as schools and families have changed, homework has become problematic for more and more students, parents, and teachers. The Internet and bookstores are crowded with books offering parents advice on how to get children to do homework. Frequently, the advice for parents is to "remain positive," yet only a handful of books suggest that parents should have the right to question the amount of homework or the value of the task itself. Teachers, overwhelmed by an already glutted curriculum and pressures related to standardized tests, assign homework in an attempt to develop students' skills and to extend learning time. At the same time, they are left frustrated when the students who most need more time to learn seem the least likely to complete homework. Teachers are afraid not to give homework, for fear of being perceived as "easy."

With diversity among learners in our schools at levels that are higher than ever, many teachers continue to assign the same homework to all students in the class and continue to disproportionately fail students from lower-income households for not doing homework, in essence punishing them for lack of an adequate environment in which to do homework. At a time when demand for accountability has reached a new high in its intensity, research fails to prove that all that homework is worth all that trouble. (The research on homework is discussed in Chapter 3.)

Although many people remain staunchly in favor of homework, a growing number of teachers and parents alike are beginning to question the practice. These critics are reexamining the beliefs behind the practice, the wisdom of assigning hours of homework, the absurdly heavy backpack, and the failure that can result when some students don't complete homework. There's a growing suspicion that something is wrong with homework.

This more critical look at homework represents a movement away from the pro-homework attitudes that have been consistent over the last two decades (Kralovec & Buell, 2000). As a result, a discussion of homework stirs controversy as people debate both sides of the issue. But the arguments both for and against homework are not new, as indicated by a consistent swing of the pendulum over the last hundred years between pro-homework and anti-homework attitudes.

A Brief History of Homework

The history of homework and surrounding attitudes is relevant because the roots of homework dogma developed and became entrenched over the last 100 years. Attitudes toward homework have historically reflected societal trends and the prevailing educational philosophy of the time, and each swing of the pendulum is colored by unique historical events and sentiments that drove the movement for or against homework. Yet the historical arguments for and against homework are familiar. They bear a striking similarity to the arguments waged in today's debate over homework.

At the end of the 19th century, attendance in the primary grades 1 through 4 was irregular for many students, and most classrooms were multiage. Teachers rarely gave homework to primary students (Gill & Schlossman, 2004). By the 5th grade, many students left school for work; fewer continued to high school (Kralovec & Buell, 2000). In the lower grades, school focused on reading, writing, and arithmetic; in grammar school (grades 5 through 8) and high school, students studied geography, history, literature, and math. Learning consisted of drill, memorization, and recitation, which required preparation at home:

> At a time when students were required to say their lessons in class in order to demonstrate their academic prowess, they had little alternative but to say those lessons over and over at home the night before. Before a child could continue his or her schooling through grammar school, a family had to decide that chores and other family obligations would not interfere unduly with the predictable nightly homework hours that would go into preparing the next day's lessons. (Gill & Schlossman, 2004, p. 174)

Given the critical role that children played as workers in the household, it was not surprising that many families could not afford to have their children continue schooling, given the requisite two to three hours of homework each night (Kralovec & Buell, 2000).

Early in the 20th century, in concert with the rise of progressive education, an anti-homework movement would become the centerpiece of the progressive platform. Progressive educators questioned many aspects of schooling: "Once the value of drill, memorization, and recitation was opened to debate, the attendant need for homework came under harsh scrutiny as well" (Kralovec & Buell, 2000, p. 42).

As pediatrics grew as a medical specialty, more doctors began to speak out about the effect of homework on the health and well-being of children. The benefits of fresh air, sunshine, and exercise for children were widely accepted, and homework had the potential to interfere. One hundred years ago, rather than diagnosing children with attention deficit disorder, pediatricians simply prescribed more outdoor exercise. Homework was blamed for nervous conditions in children, eyestrain, stress, lack of sleep, and other conditions. Homework was viewed as a culprit that robbed children of important opportunities for social interaction. At the same time, labor leaders were protesting working hours and working conditions for adults, advocating for a 40-hour workweek. Child labor laws were used as a justification to protect children from excessive homework.

In 1900, the editor of the *Ladies' Home Journal,* Edward Bok, began a series of anti-homework articles. He recommended the elimination of homework for all students under the age of 15 and a limit of one hour nightly for older students. His writings were instrumental in the growth of the anti-homework movement of the early 1900s, a harbinger of the important role media would play in the homework debate in the future. By 1930, the anti-homework sentiment had grown so strong that a Society for the Abolition of Homework was formed. Many school districts across the United States voted to abolish homework, especially in the lower grades:

In the 1930s and 1940s, although few districts abolished homework outright, many abolished it in grades K–6. In grades K–3,
condemnation of homework was nearly universal in school district policies as well as professional opinion. And even where
homework was not abolished, it was often assigned only in small
amounts—in secondary schools as well as elementary schools.
(Gill & Schlossman, 2000, p. 32)

After the Soviet Union launched the *Sputnik 1* satellite in 1957,
the trend toward less homework was quickly reversed as the
United States became obsessed with competing with the Russians.
Fearful that children were unprepared to compete in a future that
would be increasingly dominated by technology, school officials,
teachers, and parents saw homework as a means for accelerating
children's acquisition of knowledge.

The homework problem was reconceived as part of a national
crisis: the U.S. was losing the Cold War because Russian children were smarter; that is, they were working harder and achiev-
ing more in school . . . the new discourse pronounced too little
homework an indicator of the dismal state of American schooling. A commitment to heavy homework loads was alleged to
reveal seriousness of purpose in education; homework became
an instrument of national defense policy. (Gill & Schlossman,
2004, p. 176)

Within a few short years, public opinion had swung back to the
pro-homework position. During this period, many schools over-
turned policies abolishing or limiting homework that had been
established between 1900 and 1940. However, homework in the
early elementary grades was still rare (Gill & Schlossman, 2004).

By the late 1960s and early 1970s, in the midst of the Vietnam
War and the civil rights movement, a counterculture emerged that
questioned the status quo in literally every aspect of personal
and political life. A popular book, *Teaching as a Subversive Activity* (Postman & Weingartner, 1969), attacked traditional methods

of what was labeled "the educational establishment." Indicative of the times, a new debate emerged over homework and other educational activities. The anti-homework arguments were reminiscent of the progressive arguments of the early 20th century—again, homework was seen as a symptom of too much pressure on students to achieve.

Two prominent educational organizations went on record opposing excessive homework. The American Educational Research Association stated,

> Whenever homework crowds out social experience, outdoor recreation, and creative activities, and whenever it usurps time that should be devoted to sleep, it is not meeting the basic needs of children and adolescents. (In Wildman, 1968, p. 204)

The National Education Association issued this statement in 1966:

> It is generally recommended (a) that children in the early elementary school have no homework specifically assigned by the teacher; (b) that limited amounts of homework—not more than an hour a day—be introduced during the upper elementary school and junior high years; (c) that homework be limited to four nights a week; and (d) that in secondary school no more than one and a half hours a night be expected. (In Wildman, 1968, p. 204)

Not surprisingly, by the late 1960s and during the 1970s, parents were arguing that children should be free to play and relax in the evenings, and again the amount of homework decreased (Bennett & Kalish, 2006).

But by the 1980s the pendulum would swing again. In 1983, the study *A Nation at Risk* became the "first major report by the government attempting to prove that the purported inadequacies of our schools and our students were responsible for the troubles of the U.S. economy" (Kralovec & Buell, 2000, p. 50). The report claimed there was a "rising tide of mediocrity" in schools and that a movement for academic excellence was needed (National Commission on Excellence in Education, 1983). *A Nation at Risk* planted the seed of the idea that school success was responsible for economic success. It ratcheted up the standards, starting what has been called the "intensification movement"—the idea that education can be improved if only there is more of it, in the form of longer school years, more testing, more homework. *A Nation at Risk* explicitly called for "far more homework" for high school students.

In 1986, the U.S. Department of Education published *What Works,* which also recommended homework as an effective learning strategy. "Whenever you come across a particularly savage attack on the state of public education, it's a safe bet that a call for more homework (and other get-tough messages) will be sounded as well" (Kohn, 2006, p. 120).

The pro-homework trend continued into the 1990s, as the push for higher standards resulted in the conclusion that more homework was a remedy. As noted earlier, this was not the first time homework became the scapegoat for the perceived inadequacies of public education:

> Whenever reformers attempt to improve the academic outcomes of American schooling, more homework seems a first step. The justification for this probably has more to do with philosophy (students should work harder) and with the ease of implementation (increased homework costs no extra money and requires no major program modifications) than with new research findings. (Strother, in Connors, 1992, p. 14)

During the late 1980s and the early 1990s, an occasional journal article would question whether more homework was necessarily better, but those voices were few and far between. Most journal articles and popular books about homework took the safe position of being pro-homework and focused on strategies for getting children to complete homework. In 1989, Harris Cooper (now considered a leading expert on homework research) published an exhaustive synthesis of research on homework (1989a) that seemed to have little effect on popular practice and received little media attention. In 1994, a board member in the school district of Half Moon Bay, California, made national news by recommending that the district abolish homework. The board member "was widely vilified in the national press as just another California kook" (Gill & Schlossman, 1996, p. 57). The general media reaction was dismissive; the story was handled as cute and quirky, as if the idea of abolishing homework were just plain crazy.

By the late 1990s, however, the tide would begin to shift back to an anti-homework focus. With increasing frequency, articles critical of traditional homework practices were published in educational journals. In 1998, the American Educational Research Association conducted a symposium on homework practices. In 1998, Harris Cooper's latest research about homework (Cooper, Lindsay, Nye, & Greathouse, 1998) garnered much more public attention, catapulting the topic of homework into the popular press and landing him on *Oprah* and *Today*. In March 1998, the cover of *Newsweek* featured an article titled "Does Your Child Need a Tutor?" along with another article titled "Homework Doesn't Help" (Begley, 1998). In January 1999, *Time* magazine's cover story, "The Homework That Ate My Family" (Ratnesar, 1999), generated considerable media buzz. It portrayed homework as an intrusion on family tranquility and as just one more stressor in an already overstressed life, especially for two-career families. The article also cited a University of Michigan study showing that homework for 6- to 8-year-olds had increased by more than 50 percent from 1981 to 1997.

As homework increased, especially for the youngest students, and parents began feeling overwhelmed, stories detailing the struggle appeared widely in the popular press. Now the mood was one of concern for overworked students and parents. In 2000, Piscataway, New Jersey, received national attention for implementing a homework policy that limited the amount of homework, discouraged weekend homework, and forbade teachers from counting homework in the grade (Kohn, 2006). Unlike the story about Half Moon Bay only six years earlier, *this* story was given serious media coverage, and the school district was deluged by requests from schools seeking a copy of the policy.

Also in 2000, Etta Kralovec and John Buell's book *The End of Homework: How Homework Disrupts Families, Overburdens Children, and Limits Learning* received massive media attention and spawned an ongoing debate between the anti-homework and pro-homework contingents. In 2006, two popular-press books kept the debate going: Kohn's *The Homework Myth: Why Our Kids Get Too Much of a Bad Thing,* and Bennett and Kalish's *The Case Against Homework: How Homework Is Hurting Our Children and What We Can Do About It.* Since then, the debate has continued with arguments similar to those first heard in the 1930s and 1960s. Like religion and politics, the arguments for and against homework stir intense emotions among parents, teachers, and administrators. To fully understand today's debate, we must first examine the beliefs about homework that have developed over the last 100 years and the cultural forces that have shaped them.

Laying Bare the Culture of Homework

Beliefs about the inherent goodness of homework are so entrenched, so unshakable for many parents and educators, they seem almost cultlike. For many, these beliefs are unexamined. Kralovec and Buell (2000) said it best: "The belief in the value of homework is akin to faith" (p. 9). The true believers hold homework in such reverence, many educators are afraid to recommend that we eliminate it completely. Too many people just won't accept the idea. How can anyone be against work? It's as if the tradition of homework has been so romanticized as to be accepted as truth. Parenting magazines and newspaper articles accept without question that homework is part of school life and then continue to give advice on how to help kids complete it (Kohn, 2006). Freelance writers have learned that writing that is too anti-homework will probably not be published in the mainstream media.

To understand the *cult*ure of homework and how it developed over the last 100 years, it is necessary to dissect the dogma, which can best be summarized by five largely unexamined beliefs about children and learning. How many of these beliefs are based on fact, and how many are based on faith, tradition, or moral judgments?

Belief #1: The role of the school is to extend learning beyond the classroom. Many believe it is not only the inalienable right of teachers but their *obligation* to extend learning beyond the classroom. Inherent in this belief is the assumption that teachers have the *right* to control children's lives outside the school—that we have the right to give homework and that students and parents should comply with our wishes (more about this assumption in Chapter 2). Many teachers claim that homework keeps children out of trouble and that homework is better for children than television or video games. This view is rather dismissive of the judgment of parents to make good decisions about their child's use of free time. Is it really our job to be the moral policeman for our students' personal lives?

Perhaps our role in extending learning outside the school is to instill in students the value of learning and the joy of learning, and to expose them to the vastness of the universe—how much there is to learn. Perhaps our role is to help students find something in life they feel passionate about and to help them find their purpose in society.

Belief #2: Intellectual activity is intrinsically more valuable than nonintellectual activity. Many homework advocates believe that intellectual development is more important than social, emotional, or physical development. Intellectual pursuits hold an implied superiority over nonintellectual tasks such as throwing a ball, walking a dog, riding a bike, or just hanging out. This belief presupposes the limited value of leisure tasks. Concurrently, some worry that too much unstructured time might cause children to be less successful, less competitive with others. As with Belief #1, this view shows a distrust of parents to guide children in the productive use of free time and a distrust of children to engage in intellectual pursuits on their own. In reality, physical, emotional, and social activities are as necessary as intellectual activity in the development of healthy, well-rounded children.

Belief #3: Homework teaches responsibility. One of the most resilient beliefs is that homework promotes responsibility and discipline. Even though there is no research to support this belief, many people continue to tout homework's nonacademic virtues (Kohn, 2006). *Responsibility* is often a code word for *obedience.* When we say we want students to be *responsible,* are we saying we want them to be *obedient*—to do *what* we want them to do *when* we want them to do it, to be mindless drones, blindly obedient to authority? One teacher said she thought not doing homework was a sign of disrespect for the teacher! When we say homework promotes discipline in students, does that mean being self-disciplined enough to do something they hate to do because it's their duty?

Many teachers are fixated on homework as *the way* to teach responsibility, as though we have no other avenues. Yet we tend to neglect all the other ways students *could* be given responsibility in the classroom—involving them in decision making about their learning, teaching them how to self-assess, letting them design learning tasks, or allowing them to help manage classroom and school facilities (Guskey & Anderman, 2008). Even in the task of homework itself, children are rarely given *responsibility* for choosing how they wish to learn, how they might show what they have learned, or how they might schedule their time for homework. True responsibility cannot be coerced. It must be developed by allowing students power and ownership of tasks (Vatterott, 2007). (Chapter 4 presents more about how to do this.)

Another supposed virtue of homework is that it teaches time management. Does time management really mean the ability to delay gratification—to work when we want to play? Homework does not reinforce time management if adults have to coerce children into doing it; if children are coerced, they are not in charge of scheduling the time or making decisions about the use of the time.

If we are using homework to teach responsibility, won't 10 minutes of homework work just as well as 60 minutes? If we are using homework to teach time management, don't long-range projects that require scheduled planning do a better job of that than daily assignments?

Belief #4: Lots of homework is a sign of a rigorous curriculum. Many people equate lots of homework with a tough school, regardless of the type or length of assignments (Jackson, 2009). Parents will often brag: "My child goes to a really good school—he gets lots of homework." If the mind is a muscle to be trained (as was believed in the 19th century), then more work must equal more learning. If some homework is good for children, then more homework must be even better. If 10 math problems for homework are good, then 40 problems must be better. This belief, more than any other, is responsible for the piling on of hours of homework in many schools today. Yet we all know that those assignments could be busywork, of no educational value (Jackson, 2009). More homework gives the *appearance* of increased rigor, and "difficulty is often equated to the *amount* of work done by students, rather than the complexity and challenge" (Williamson & Johnston, 1999, p. 10, emphasis added). Ah, if it were only that simple. More time does not necessarily equal more learning. The "more is always better" argument ignores the quality of work and the level of learning required. Rigor is challenge—but it is not necessarily the same challenge for each student. Given the diverse nature of students, challenging learning experiences will vary for different students.

Belief #5: Good teachers give homework; good students do their homework. Probably the most disturbing belief is the belief in the inherent goodness of homework, regardless of the type or length of assignment. Homework advocates have believed it for years, never questioning whether it might not be true. This belief is born from both the belief that homework teaches responsibility and discipline and the belief that "lots of homework" equals "rigor." If *good teachers give homework,* it naturally follows, then, that teachers who don't give homework are too easy. This mindset is so ingrained that teachers apologize to other teachers for not giving homework! Yet we know that some very good teachers don't give a lot of homework or give none at all. Instead of being apologetic, teachers who don't give homework should simply explain that they do such a good job of teaching that homework is not necessary.

The danger in the belief that *good students do their homework* is the moral judgment that tends to accompany this belief. To children who dutifully complete homework, we often attribute the virtues of being compliant and hardworking. To children who don't complete homework, we often attribute the vices of laziness and noncompliance. But is a lack of virtue the reason many children don't do homework? Therein lies the problem. Students without supportive parents (or with single parents overburdened trying to make ends meet), with inadequate home environments for completing homework, or with parents intellectually unable to help them are less likely to complete homework (Vatterott, 2007). Are these less advantaged students *bad?* Of course not.

These beliefs form a dogma, a homework culture. The foundations of that culture are a trinity of very old philosophies. Homework culture is a complex mix of moralistic views, puritanism, and behaviorism. The beliefs that underlie the homework dogma have been fed by our moralistic views of human nature, the puritan work ethic that is embedded in our culture, and behaviorist practices that still reside in our schools. The five beliefs and these three philosophies are so well entwined, it's hard to tell where one idea begins and another ends. An exploration of these philosophies will illuminate the foundations of the dogma that is homework culture.

Moralistic Views: Who We Believe Students Are

Historically, one mission of the school has been to instill moral values. Unfortunately, much of traditional schooling operates on the theory that children are basically lazy and irresponsible, that they can't be trusted, and that they have to be coerced into learning. They must be controlled and taught to be compliant. Therefore, it follows that it is necessary to use homework to teach responsibility.

If students naturally have a tendency to do evil, then they cannot be trusted to use time wisely. Idle hands are the devil's workshop, and therefore children should not be idle. This philosophy assumes not only that children don't want to learn but also that learning is inherently distasteful.

The Puritan Work Ethic: Who We Want Students to Be

No one would dispute that we want to encourage students to work hard. After all, hard work is what made America great, right? The Puritans believed hard work was an honor to God that would lead to a prosperous reward. That work ethic brings to mind the stereotypical stern schoolmarm, rapping a ruler against the desk and saying "Get busy!" The tenets of the puritan work ethic most evident in homework culture are the following:

- Hard work is good for you regardless of the pointlessness of the task.
- Hard works builds character.
- Hard work is painful; suffering is virtuous.

Here we see the origin of Belief #4, that more work equals rigor, and Belief #5, that "good" students do their homework and "good" teachers make students work hard. Unfortunately, when it comes to learning, the bleaker side of the puritan work ethic has also taken hold:

> There is a prevalent myth that if a teaching/learning experience is too enjoyable it is somehow academically suspect. If it is "rigorous," or better yet painful, then it must have merit. (Raebeck, 1992, p. 13)

The work ethic is obvious in views that homework is a way to train students how to work—that homework trains students how to study, how to work diligently and persistently, and how to delay gratification (Bempechat, 2004). Along similar lines, homework is also viewed as practice for being a worker:

> Homework is *work*, not play. . . . It is assigned by a teacher for students to complete on the teacher's schedule, with the teacher's requirements in mind. So it helps to have the right attitude. Homework means business, and the student should expect to buckle down. As in the workplace, careless efforts and a laissez-faire attitude are likely to make the wrong impression . . . homework is, in part, an exchange of performance for grades. (Corno & Xu, 2004, p. 228)

The premise of Corno and Xu's article is that "homework is the quintessential job of childhood"—as though children need a job. Which begs the question: Is our job as educators to produce learners or workers?

Behaviorism: How We Think We Can Control Students

No philosophy is more firmly rooted in education than behaviorism. The idea that behavior can be controlled by rewards and punishment is so embedded in the day-to-day practices of school, one rarely even notices it (Kohn, 1999). Discipline, grades, attendance policies, honor rolls, and even the way teachers use praise and disapproval—all reflect this philosophy that behavior can be controlled by external stimuli. So it's no surprise that teachers believe rewards and punishments are the way to *make* students do homework. When punishments don't work, teachers often increase the punishment, as if more of the same will accomplish the goal.

If we believe that good students do their homework and lazy students don't, then it becomes morally defensible to give failing grades for incomplete homework, thereby punishing the vice of laziness and rewarding the virtue of hard work. Behaviorism is most evident in the use of late policies and zeros for uncompleted homework (more about that in Chapter 4).

The moralistic, puritanistic, and behavioristic foundations are so firmly entrenched in homework culture, traditional homework practices may be accepted without question by both teachers and parents, as if a sort of brainwashing has occurred. To use a 1970s metaphor, "if you drank the Kool-Aid," you may not realize how the cult affects your attitudes about homework.

Forces Driving the Current Pro-Homework/ Anti-Homework Debate

Homework beliefs and their historical influences affect the debate today in insidious ways. The arguments today are strongly reminiscent of the earlier arguments for and against homework, yet something is different. This time around we face new and unique challenges.

No Child Left Behind

Never before have we lived with the specter of No Child Left Behind and the accountability it demands. The pressure to meet standards has never been more intense, and homework is seen as a tool for meeting those standards. The pressure has changed education even at the kindergarten and 1st grade levels. A *Newsweek* cover story called it the "new first grade":

> In the last decade, the earliest years of schooling have become less like a trip to "Mister Rogers' Neighborhood" and more like SAT prep. Thirty years ago first grade was for learning how to read. Now, reading lessons start in kindergarten and kids who don't crack the code by the middle of the first grade get extra help. (Tyre, 2006, p. 36)

Many parents complain that homework is now routinely assigned in kindergarten and 1st grade. YouTube hosts a now famous 911 call from a 4-year-old preschooler who needed help with his "takeaway" math homework. In the desperation to meet standards, even recess has been affected. One survey indicated that only 70 percent of kindergarten classrooms had a recess period (Pellegrini, 2005).

Media and Technology

Media and technology have broadened the homework debate to be more inclusive than in the past; more people are participating in the conversation. The Internet has given the public more information, served as a forum for many pro-homework and anti-homework blogs, and given us a window to similar debates in other countries. Today the homework debate is played out on iVillage and other parenting Web sites, as well as on radio and television and in the print media. Web sites such as www.stophomework.com (Bennett & Kalish, 2006) have united parents and given them strategies for protesting homework policies in their child's school. Technology has reduced the isolation of parents; their private homework struggles can now be vented in public with the click of a mouse.

Just as 100 years ago the *Ladies' Home Journal* writings sparked a movement, over the last decade the media have been a friend of homework reform. Since the release of Cooper's 1998 comprehensive study, major news magazines and talk shows have conducted a national dialogue about homework and have brought increased attention to the anti-homework movement. With a seemingly endless supply of television talk shows, quasi-news shows (such as *Dateline*), and round-the-clock cable news coverage, issues affecting families—including homework—have received more coverage. The availability of online media has allowed us to access that homework story on *Today* or that homework article in the *New York Times* long after publication, and without leaving our homes. Media and technology have helped to accelerate the growth of the anti-homework movement.

But the media has also been an enemy of the anti-homework movement. Every year, around back-to-school time, the media buries us with books, magazine articles, and television segments that reinforce a blind acceptance of homework as a good thing, endorsing the importance of homework and offering parents the same stale tips for getting children to do homework "without tears." Throughout the school year, stories appear frequently about how to get your son or daughter into the Ivy League, how to ace the SATs, or how to help your child write a killer college essay.

The New Mass Hysteria

All this press fuels a mass hysteria among parents about their child's ability to compete and to be successful. An American Academy of Pediatrics report labeled the trend "the professionalization of parenthood":

> Parents receive messages from a variety of sources stating that good parents actively build every skill and aptitude their child might need from the earliest ages. . . . They hear other parents in the neighborhood talk about their overburdened schedules and recognize it is the culture and even expectation of parents. (Ginsburg, 2007, p. 185)

The new mass hysteria has parents driven by fear. It's a dog-eat-dog world, and the competition is tough. If you're not careful, you won't survive. It's a high-stakes game, with your child's future on the line. For many parents, the mantra has become "do whatever it takes" to get their child accepted at the best college—all of this with a tacit acceptance of the premise that admission into Harvard equals a high-paying career, which equals happiness. As one high school student put it:

> People don't go to school to learn. They go to get good grades, which brings them to college, which brings them the high-paying job, which brings them happiness, so they think. (Pope, 2001, p. 4)

And as the superintendent in one wealthy district sardonically stated, "Our parents believe there are three career paths for their children: doctor, lawyer, and unsuccessful."

There seems to be little discussion that, in fact, this could be a faulty hypothesis, and only recently have some experts advised parents to question whether the Ivy League is right for *their* child. Three faulty assumptions actually feed this trend: (1) the Ivy League is the only route to success; (2) advanced placement (AP) classes are essential to get there; and (3) excessive homework is an inevitable part of AP or honors classes.

* * *

AP Haley

Talking with other parents at a neighborhood get-together, Haley's mom is worried. Even though Haley is a good student—taking three AP classes, active in cheerleading and other activities—her mom is worried that she is not in the top 10 percent of her class. "She's only in the top 15 percent—she can't get into the University of Texas unless she's in the top 10 percent." Her mom wishes kids today weren't so competitive and claims her daughter wants to take three AP classes. She claims she's not pushing her daughter and doesn't even realize how clearly her anxiety about the future is communicated and how readily her daughter picks it up. Mom goes on to remind the others, "Look at the jobs John's kids got when they graduated from Peabody and Georgetown—all the money they are making!"

• • •

The stress is cultural—absorbed by parents and then fed to their children, creating a hypercompetitive attitude for both parents and children:

> Parents receive the message that if their children are not well prepared, well balanced, and high achieving, they will not get a desired spot in higher education. Even parents who wish to take a lower-key approach to child rearing fear slowing down when they perceive everyone else is on the fast track. (Ginsburg, 2007, p. 185)

This trend has led many parents to have a somewhat schizophrenic attitude toward homework. They complain about the stress homework brings to children, the battles over the dinner table, and the disruption to family life, yet at the same time they are worried about their child's ability to compete for entry into the best colleges. Although never proven by research, parents assume an automatic relationship between homework and future success. They have bought into the cult of beliefs about homework and accepted a connection between hours of homework and acceptance to an elite college. (Unfortunately, the manner in which many AP courses are taught reinforces this belief.) They wrongly assume that if it takes hours of homework in high school to guarantee admission to college, so be it.

One result of the mass hysteria has been a virtual explosion of the tutoring industry, now a $6 billion business (Bennett & Kalish, 2006). Some parents use tutoring to give their college-bound children a leg up. But more often, for parents who can afford it, the answer to the stressful and time-consuming job of supervising homework has been to "subcontract" the job to a tutor.

One of the potential negative effects of the tutoring craze has been the possibility that mass tutoring may "raise the bar" for homework assignments. After all, if most students are getting adult help with homework, it gives teachers the misperception that the students know more than they really do. It makes it appear that students are ready for more challenging assignments.

The candy factory episode of the classic *I Love Lucy* sitcom comes to mind. Lucy and Ethel are hired to work on an assembly line wrapping chocolates that pass by them on a conveyor belt. Struggling to keep up with the pace, they begin taking chocolates off the conveyor and stuffing them in their mouths and their hats. When the supervisor comes to check on their progress, they appear to be keeping up, so she yells to the back, "Speed it up!" Mass tutoring has the same potential to affect the difficulty of homework assignments in wealthy communities while widening the gap between those wealthy students and disadvantaged students whose families can't afford tutors.

The Balance Movement

At the same time that some parents are mired in the mass hysteria, a backlash is occurring. Other parents are backing up and slowing down, seeking a balance in their children's lives. Although some are recommending that homework be abolished, many more are suggesting that excessive homework is interfering with family life and not worth the loss of a carefree childhood. The movement is less an anti-homework movement than an anti–excessive homework movement, based on the idea that children should not have longer than an eight-hour workday (Vatterott, 2003). As a reaction against the mass hysteria movement, these parents have decided they are unwilling to mortgage their son's or daughter's childhood for the nebulous promise of future success. Nearly 30 years ago, David Elkind warned about *The Hurried Child* (1981)—a trend to push children too hard, to overstructure their time, and to burden them with too many adult responsibilities. Today's balance movement echoes that concern, and it is continuing to gain support among teachers, other professionals, and the general public.

In 2007, the American Academy of Pediatrics released a report indicating the importance of undirected playtime for children (Ginsburg, 2007). The report addressed the tendencies of parents to overschedule and "build résumés" for children, and the negative ramifications of such actions. The report stated that play not only enhances social and emotional development but also helps to maintain parent-child bonds. It also recommended that pediatricians encourage active play and discourage parents from the overuse of passive entertainment for children (such as television and computer games). Some parents have already heeded this advice. With the ability of children to be connected and stimulated 24/7, some parents are now beginning to limit screen time and force kids to take "media fasts." A worldwide Slow Movement, for both children and adults, is catching on and is documented in the book *In Praise of Slowness: Challenging the Cult of Speed* (Honore, 2004). The London-based author claims that the Slow Movement can help people live happier, healthier, and more productive lives by slowing down their pace.

Parents who feel strongly about the need for balance are concerned about both immediate and long-term effects of homework engulfing their children's free time. The immediate effects are simple—loss of leisure time, stress, and overall health.

Loss of leisure time. Parents often remark that, because of excessive homework, children are "losing their childhood" and "don't have time to be kids." They point to the need for fresh air, unstructured playtime, family time, and downtime. Their concerns are supported by recent brain research showing the importance of downtime and rest for peak learning efficiency (Jensen, 2000).

Stress. The stress levels of school-age children are another concern. "This hurried lifestyle is a source of stress and anxiety and may even contribute to depression" (Ginsburg, 2007, p. 185). While some are recommending children's yoga and meditation as a way to cope with stress, others are targeting the sources of stress, and homework is a major culprit. Pediatricians and counselors report many stress-related symptoms, such as stomachaches and headaches, related to children's anxiety over their inability to complete homework. In an acknowledgment of the stress experienced by high school students, Stanford University now sponsors a program called Challenge Success (formerly called Stressed Out Students [SOS]) that works with school teams composed of the principal, students, parents, counselors, and teachers or other adults (Pope, 2005). The program helps schools implement school-level strategies known to improve students' mental and physical health and engagement in school.

Overall health. And finally, parents are concerned about the effect of excessive homework on the overall physical and psychological health of children. The traditional practice of assigning homework in every subject every night and the antiquated reliance on textbooks as curriculum have led to a physical problem. The weight of the backpack has been a subject of concern for some time, with an increasing number of students complaining of back pain (Galley, 2001). The American Chiropractic Association, the American Physical Therapy Association, and the American Academy of Orthopedic Surgeons all recommend that the weight of backpacks not exceed 15 percent of the child's body weight (Moore, White, & Moore, 2007). Yet in one study of students in grades 5 to 8, more than half the students interviewed said they regularly carried backpack loads that were heavier than 15 percent of their body weight, and roughly one-third of the students interviewed had a history of back pain (Galley, 2001). Research done more recently now supports the recommendation that 10 percent of body weight be the cutoff for safe use of backpacks at all grade levels. The problem has doctors so concerned that, beginning in 2005, the American Occupational Therapy Association has sponsored a National School Backpack Awareness Day each September. Researchers recommend that schools review homework policies to reduce the necessity of carrying textbooks home (Moore et al., 2007).

Many children sacrifice fresh air, exercise, or sleep to toil over hours of homework. Recent alarming news about the level of childhood obesity, the negative effects of sleep deprivation, and the established connection between sleep deprivation and obesity add strong arguments to the move to reduce homework to allow for more exercise and sleep. One child advocacy expert has compiled cutting-edge research showing that direct exposure to nature is essential for healthy physical, emotional, and spiritual development. He warns that today's overworked and overscheduled children can suffer from what he calls *nature deficit disorder,* resulting in obesity, depression, and attention deficit disorder (Louv, 2005).

Love of learning. In addition to these short-term effects, parents are also concerned about homework's long-term effect on children. In educational circles, discussion almost exclusively focuses on short-term achievement or passing the test, not on what the practice of homework does to a child's long-term learning, attitude about learning, or attitudes about the intellectual life. But parents are worried about the potential of excessive homework to dampen their child's natural curiosity, passion, and love of learning. Their concern, as stated by Alfie Kohn, is that homework may be "the single most reliable extinguisher of the flame of curiosity" (2006, p. 17).

Summing Up

Historically, the homework debate has continued to repeat itself. But the flawed belief system that homework is grounded on has yet to be adequately challenged. What complicates today's debate is the diversity of attitudes about the value of homework. The mass hysteria and balance movements illustrate the breadth of those attitudes. The pendulum is swinging both ways at the same time. As a country, the United States is so diverse economically, culturally, and in parenting styles, it is not surprising that not all would agree on a practice that bridges both school and family life. This diversity of attitudes requires not only a critical examination of homework practices but also a rethinking of the school-family relationship. This topic is discussed in Chapter 2.

2

Homework in the Context of the New Family

Homework occurs within the context of both school and family, but the traditional practices of homework may be out of sync with the needs of today's families. The incredible diversity among families presents many challenges to the successful implementation of homework. Families are more economically and culturally diverse than in the past, and family composition is more varied than ever before, with divorced parents and blended families increasingly common, and with more grandparents than ever raising their grandchildren. Today's families exhibit a variety of parenting styles and values, some of which may be mismatched with the values of teachers and schools.

In previous generations, mainstream America seemed to agree about issues like honesty, respecting authority, obeying the law, premarital sex, and child rearing. Children received similar messages about right and wrong from their school, church, home, and neighborhood. If it takes a village to raise a child, in previous generations the village *was* raising the child. Adults seemed to agree about what was best for children. In some communities today, those shared values still exist, but in other communities that consistency of message is sorely lacking (Taffel, 2001).

The 1960s "do your own thing" generation marked the beginning of a diversity of family and societal values that continues to widen. As our society grows more diverse, students and parents may no longer receive the same messages from their family, church, community, and school. Parents value their individuality and freedom to set their own standards about child rearing. The result is that today there is little standardization among parents about child rearing (Tell, 2000). A broad diversity of opinions exists about such things as whether children should attend church, be paid for chores, or have curfews. Mainstream America cannot agree on whether children should be spanked, what clothing is too sexy for adolescent girls, or how much supervision children should have (Vatterott, 2007). On almost any given parenting topic, it is difficult for a group of parents to reach consensus. Regardless of how similar parents in a school appear to be, it is unlikely that all will have the same opinions about parenting or how homework should be handled.

Economic diversity, cultural diversity, and different parenting styles and family values converge to have an effect on homework, creating differing views of the parent-school relationship and differing attitudes about homework. A diversity in family values makes it even more likely that those values will clash with the values of individual teachers. Can we teach without judging the values of our students' families? It is important for educators to understand the complexity of today's families and to respect individual family values when implementing homework as an instructional practice.

Diversity of Parenting Styles

The evolution of democracy, in the United States and around the world, has profoundly affected families. Children, once viewed as powerless, are gaining legal rights and protections once reserved only for adults (Vatterott, 2007). This shift has influenced power relationships within families; traditional power relationships have given way to more democratic, egalitarian relationships between parents and children.

This generation of children is the most democratically raised in U.S. history—protected by law against abuse and neglect and often allowed to make decisions at an early age about what they eat and wear, and what toys their parents buy. As U.S. culture has become more democratic, a diversity of power relationships has emerged among families. A significant change in parenting style that affects homework has been the trend away from authoritative parenting and toward more democratic families. One might call it "the death of the dictatorship" in parenting.

Parenting a dictatorship? To understand the analogy, one need only listen to adults who grew up in the 1950s talk about their childhood. Many of them will remark that "children didn't have rights" in that day. Children did what they were told, ate whatever food was put in front of them, and wore the clothes their parents picked out for them. They did their homework because they were told to. The parent-child relationship was definitely top-down, and children were relatively powerless. This traditional power structure still exists in some families and in some cultures today, but it is not as prevalent as it once was. When teachers say, "Why can't the parents just *make* their children do their homework?" they may be visualizing a dictatorial style of parenting that no longer exists in those families.

In many families, parental control of children has become less absolute. Many parents today have vowed not to be the dictators their parents were. They have allowed their children to have input into decisions, and they have often negotiated compromises with their children. More traditional parents (and more traditional teachers) will claim *that* is the problem with homework—that children have been given the impression that everything is negotiable and that parents have allowed children to be in charge. In a few families, parents may have lost a clear sense of their authority, and children may have learned how to be in control. But in most families, parents are firmly in charge even though children have input into decisions.

How does parenting style affect homework? Rather than controlling all aspects of their child's life, parents who are not dictators are much more likely to choose their battles. Unfortunately, homework has become a big battle in many families. One study indicated that half of the parents surveyed had a serious argument with their child about homework over the last year (Kohn, 2006). Many parents are tired of the tension, the teary battles at the kitchen table, and the nagging they have to do to get the homework completed. They do not want to be the teacher's enforcer, the "homework cop" (Bennett & Kalish, 2006). Frustrated by their inability to force their children to do boring tasks or to continue to work when they are tired, many parents have decided that homework is not a battle they want to fight. When asked what she thought about problems with homework, one family counselor said, "The problem with homework is that parents are wimps" (meaning that they are no longer dictators). Maybe parents are not wimps; maybe they are smarter than we give them credit for. Maybe they realize the lack of value of some homework tasks, and maybe they know their children well enough to know when they need downtime.

Diversity of Beliefs About the Place of Academic Work in Life

Parents also differ in their beliefs about the place of academic work in a balanced life. Parents of all socioeconomic levels have a variety of opinions about the importance of homework in their child's daily life and what the balance should be between homework and other activities. Again, these beliefs may not be compatible with teacher beliefs.

All Academics, All the Time

Some parents believe that homework is the avenue through which all virtue flows. To them, academic life is the priority—as Corno

(1996) believes: "Homework is the job of childhood." For children in the All Academics, All the Time families, homework totally defines a child's free time. These parents believe homework is one way they can help their child get ahead and that it is the path to lifetime achievement (Kralovec & Buell, 2000). At a parent meeting in which school officials were discussing a new policy limiting homework, one parent asked, "Well, then, what would they do with their time?" Part of the rationale for All Academics, All the Time is the belief, discussed in Chapter 1, that intellectual activity is intrinsically more valuable than nonintellectual pursuits and that homework is better than television or video games. This attitude indicates a false sense of security that homework will somehow keep children out of trouble, away from vices like sex, alcohol, and drugs. The All Academics, All the Time mind-set lacks an understanding of the value of play, leisure pursuits, and downtime in a child's physical, intellectual, and psychological development (Crain, 2003).

All Academics, All the Time parents often ask for extra homework for their child and become nervous when there is no homework to fill weekends and vacations. They seem to assume that as long as their kids have homework to do every night—never mind what it is—then learning must be taking place. Educational quality is assumed to be synonymous with rigor, and rigor, in turn, is thought to be reflected by the quantity and difficulty of assignments (Kohn, 2006, p. 20). If teachers have no suggestions for enrichment activities, these parents will often create homework for their children, making them study or review previous work.

Balancing Academics and Family-Chosen Activities

Another group of parents wishes to balance homework with other outside activities they and their child have chosen. These parents often claim they want their child to be well rounded, while some are also feeding the high school résumé to enhance their child's college opportunities. Whatever the reason, many children are involved in numerous outside activities after school.

Teachers may feel entitled to counsel parents on the over-scheduling of their child, but this is a slippery slope. It is certainly within our jurisdiction to recommend that students take fewer advanced placement classes (if we feel that taking those classes is contributing to homework overload), or to be concerned if students appear exhausted or overly stressed. But we must be careful that we truly have the best interest of the child in mind, rather than just wanting to see homework completed.

Parents have the right to control their child's time outside school. Parents frequently complain about students being forced to miss activities such as scout meetings or piano lessons because of excessive homework. Religious, cultural, or family traditions must also be respected. In some communities, homework is not assigned on Wednesday evenings because so many children attend church that evening. Many parents would like their children to attend an evening Bible study class one night a week. Catholic students who attend public school may take religion classes one evening a week in preparation for First Communion or Confirmation. In many cultures, Saturday or Sunday is designated as family day, when time spent with family takes priority over schoolwork. These examples offer just a few reasons to eliminate homework on weekends or during vacations.

Balancing Academics, Leisure, and Happiness

Many parents simply feel their children's lives are too busy and would like them to have more leisure time. "They just need time to play," "We just want them to be able to do nothing sometime," "It would be nice to have time to hang out with our kids and maybe watch a television show together," parents will say. They instinctively realize that their children's lives are too hectic, that their children are not relaxed or are not getting adequate sleep. One parent of a 6th grader in a gifted program complained that her daughter had two to three hours of homework a night. "The attitude of the teacher and administration seems to be that 'if she can't do the work maybe she doesn't belong here.' We are torn between wanting the challenge of the program and concern for our daughter's overall well-being."

Parents are also concerned about the stress that homework brings to children's daily routine. Some young children are exhausted after school and struggle to complete any homework at all. These are children who fairly recently were still taking naps in the afternoon (Kohn, 2006). Empathic parents and authors Bennett and Kalish (2006) provide a metaphor:

> For many kids, homework is like having to do their taxes *every night*. How would we feel if we came home to hours of work from five different bosses? At least some of us would quit or enter therapy—which is where some of our children now find themselves. (p. 22)

Divorced parents and parents with unusual work schedules also have concerns. Many noncustodial divorced parents complain that they see their child only a few hours a week, and they don't want to spend that time fighting over homework. Parents who work evenings or do shift work may have only occasional blocks of time to spend with their child, and when they do, they want it to be relaxed, enjoyable time. Is it any wonder that for these families quality time takes precedence over homework?

The Priority of Family Responsibilities and Paid Work

For some children, especially those from low-income families, time after school is a precious resource for a family stretched thin. Those children's families may need them to babysit younger siblings, cook meals, do laundry, or clean. For families who own businesses or farms, children are a valuable part of the workforce. (How often do you see school-age children helping out in small family-owned restaurants?) In these situations, homework could actually be taking money out of the family's pocket. For example, at one Wisconsin middle school, a mandatory after-school program required students to make up missing homework assignments. The program had prevented many students from failing and had been well received. However, one parent complained that the program had cost her $210 that month for babysitting because her son was staying after school. This frustrated the administrator, who felt good that the boy was no longer failing. But to that parent, the financial priority was more critical than the incomplete homework. Again, family values sometimes conflict with the values of the school.

Even when the financial need is not dire, many families believe strongly in the value of paid work. As soon as their children are old enough to work, they expect them to start building an employment record. This is viewed as a legitimate method of teaching responsibility and money management, as well as preparation for a future life in the workforce. Whether students actually *need* to work is irrelevant to us as educators. It is the family value driving the decision that must be respected.

What does all this mean for homework? This diversity of family values, family priorities, and individual differences in students renders the one-size-fits-all homework plan virtually useless. Some parents will want more homework; some will want less. Some students will succeed with very full schedules, whereas others will thrive only when given adequate downtime to de-stress. This diversity of daily life after school also speaks volumes to the antiquated practice of assigning homework at 3:00 p.m. on Tuesday and expecting it back at 8:00 a.m. on Wednesday. Teachers need to accept that on certain evenings it will be impossible for some students to complete homework. Teachers must be careful not to focus so intensely on learning that they lose sight of the importance of family life. Teachers will need to remain flexible about family priorities and also learn more about their individual students' schedules outside school. Many teachers have replaced daily homework with monthly or weekly lists, or a course syllabus showing all homework assignments for the semester. This approach allows more flexibility for the students and allows them to plan ahead for conflicts.

Diversity of Parental Involvement in Homework

Parents' involvement in the homework process can run the gamut from no involvement at all to regularly completing their children's homework for them. That involvement may differ due to the age of the student, the ability level of the student, the educational level of the parent, and the time the parent has available.

At one end of the continuum are parents who do not get involved at all with their child's homework. They don't ask if their child has homework, nor do they check to see if it is completed. They may care about their child's education but simply do not have the time, energy, or opportunity to be involved. Many parents are uninvolved because they have made a conscious decision to take a hands-off approach. Many have stopped being involved with homework because they are tired of the battle. They don't *want* the job, and they don't think it should *be* their job. As one parent said, "Teachers want us to do their job. Parents should not be expected to morph into tutors by night." Those parents feel it is the teacher's job to work with the student to ensure that homework is completed. Uninvolved parents will often say, "If it's supposed to help the child be responsible, why is it *my* job?" Many parents of high school students, in an effort to help their children be more independent, have stopped supervising homework. How do uninvolved parents feel about their lack of involvement? Some are quite comfortable, some are resentful that they are *expected* to be involved, and some feel guilty that they are being judged as bad parents.

On the other end of the continuum are the overinvolved parents, nicknamed "helicopter parents" because of their tendency to hover over their child's education, scrutinizing every move of the teacher and the student (Kantrowitz & Tyre, 2006). These are the parents who often micromanage homework and won't hesitate to do homework for the child to ensure a good grade. Why do these parents micromanage? There could be several reasons: being fearful of the child's failing, overprotecting the child from unpleasantness, or saving the child from pain by not allowing the child to make mistakes. Punitive grading practices inadvertently encourage this overinvolvement from parents.

Many of these parental behaviors are self-imposed—you will often hear parents say, "I need to make sure the homework is right," "I feel I must be involved," "If I don't help them, they will fail," and "I know I shouldn't do the work for them, but I just can't help myself." Do these statements sound a little obsessive-compulsive? As any psychologist will tell you, this kind of behavior is often driven by the desire to reduce anxiety—in this case, parental anxiety spurred on by the mass hysteria about their children's future that was discussed in Chapter 1.

Unfortunately, this classic enabling behavior often does more harm than good. By micromanaging and taking responsibility for homework, these parents risk discouraging their children's self-reliance and may even rob the children of their own sense of accomplishment. Parents also send a message to their children that they don't trust them to do the work. The children quickly learn that if they act helpless, their parents will do the job for them. This may seem like protective and compassionate behavior on the part of parents, but it eventually backfires when children get to middle school and high school.

Some parents will say that it's necessary to be so involved, that homework has changed and become more complex (Bennett & Kalish, 2006). Is homework today really so different? If homework is so complex that students cannot complete it on their own, that is a problem that should be addressed with the teacher, not by doing the work for the child. But many parents seem unwilling or unable to discuss homework with teachers, afraid to question if the amount or difficulty of homework assignments is right for their child. They accept that this homework must be what needs to be done.

Economic Diversity Issues:
The "Haves" and the "Have-Nots"

Economic diversity of families holds perhaps the greatest challenge as schools struggle to implement fair and equitable homework policies. There appears to be an ever-widening chasm between the rich and the poor (Zuckerman, 2006), which has major implications for education in general and homework in particular. One indication of this trend is that between 1995 and 2004, families headed by college graduates showed a 75.8 percent *increase* in net worth, whereas families headed by high school dropouts showed a *decrease* of 26.2 percent (Pethokoukis, 2006).

> America is fast becoming a nation of haves and have-nots, with rising income inequality. Data from the Federal Reserve for 2001 to 2004 shows that median family income rose just 1.6 percent during that period, compared with 9.5 percent during 1998 to 2001. Income distribution from 1995 to 2004, during both an economic boom and a recession, kept tilting toward the already wealthy. The top income quartile gained 77 percent, while the bottom gained just 8 percent. (Pethokoukis, 2006, p. 43)

Socioeconomic status separates the haves from the have-nots in several concrete ways, all of which can affect learning. The works of Betty Hart and Todd Risley (1995) and Richard Rothstein (2004) document important gaps between the home environments of lower-class students and students from the middle or upper class. First, there is a *reading gap*—lower-class students may not have books in the home, are less likely to be read to in the home, and are less likely to see their parents reading for pleasure or reading to solve problems. Second, there is a *conversation gap*—professional parents speak more than twice as many words per hour to their children than do welfare parents. By the age of 3, children of professional parents have a vocabulary twice as large as that of welfare children (Hart & Risley, 1995). And third, there is a *health and housing gap*—lower-class students, in general, are in poorer health than middle- or upper-class students. As a result of poorer prenatal conditions, unhealthy environments, and lack of medical care, lower-class students are more likely to have vision problems, dental problems, and asthma. Because they often lack health insurance, they are more likely to miss school for minor health problems that go untreated, such as ear infections. All of these factors put lower-class children at a disadvantage, even before they enter school (Rothstein, 2004).

For children with special needs, class differences are especially important because they often influence the amount and quality of learning assistance these children receive. Consider the following examples of Sydney and Dillon, two 3rd grade boys with learning disabilities.

Sydney is from a lower-class family. His parents are both high school dropouts and understand little about the concept of learning disabilities. They know Sydney has always struggled in school, but they have trouble taking time off from their jobs to talk to the teacher. They feel uncomfortable talking to people at the school and do not know it is possible for Sydney to be tested for a learning disability or to receive special help. They cannot afford to send Sydney to a tutor. Sydney lags far behind the other 3rd graders in reading and math.

Dillon also has a learning disability, but his story is much different. His parents are wealthy and highly educated. Before kindergarten, they participated in a school-sponsored parenting program, which taught them how to enhance Dillon's cognitive development. When he performed poorly on the kindergarten screening, they paid to have a comprehensive assessment done through a child development center at a local hospital. Dillon's parents had him tested by the school in kindergarten, advocated for special placement with the best teachers, and closely monitored his progress. Dillon and his parents regularly see a family counselor, and Dillon gets weekly help from a tutor. As a result, in the 3rd grade Dillon is close to grade level in reading and math.

As the stories illustrate, class differences can easily create disadvantages at school for lower-class children. Unfortunately, homework has the potential to exacerbate class differences and widen the achievement gap. Kralovec and Buell (2000) describe the problem succinctly: "Homework appears to further disadvantage the already disadvantaged" (p. 70). In the worst-case scenario, homework helps the privileged succeed academically, and homework causes the less privileged to fail academically. Sadly, Kralovec and Buell (2000) found that the inability to keep up with homework was a critical factor in the decision of lower-class students to drop out of school. Consider the lives of the following three high school students—Emma, Ashley, and Maria—and how their families' economic situations affect their ability to complete homework.

Even when Emma has several hours of homework, she always completes it. Her parents take pride in how hard she works, convinced that rigorous homework will prepare Emma for an Ivy League education. Emma's parents both have advanced degrees, and they often have intellectual discussions with Emma about the subjects she is studying. They have an extensive home library, Internet access, and plenty of money to hire tutors and purchase materials for homework projects. Emma has her own computer. In her pursuit of the perfect grade point average, Emma has learned how to cut corners and even cheat when necessary, and how to do without sleep and a social life in order to be a successful student (Pope, 2001).

Ashley usually does her homework. Although her parents are not highly educated, they value education, and it is important to them that Ashley do well in school. Both her parents work long hours, and their free time is often consumed with household chores. Though their schedules seem overwhelming, Ashley's parents usually find time to monitor her homework but often do not understand the content. Sometimes they drive her to the store for homework materials. The family has one computer that several people must share. Ashley's parents usually check to make sure Ashley has done her homework.

Maria often does not do her homework. She comes home immediately after school three days a week to care for her younger siblings so her single mother can go to work. The other two days, Maria works part-time after school to supplement her mother's paycheck. Even when she has time, circumstances make it difficult for her to complete homework. There is no quiet place in the house to study, and there is no computer. Maria's mother has only a 6th grade education and does not speak English very well, so it is hard for her to help Maria with homework. The family budget has no money for materials for homework projects. Even if money were available, the family has no car for the trip to the store. It is not safe to walk to the public library.

Obviously these scenarios do not represent all students—not all upper-class students are like Emma and Dillon, and not all lower-class students are like Sydney and Maria. Although differences in homework completion exist among students regardless of social class, the scenarios illustrate the discrepancy in the homework experience that *can* occur across social classes. For poor families, homework may be a low priority compared to survival (Payne, 2001). If those parents feel that school has not benefited them in their lives, they may see homework as a waste of time in view of the more essential needs of preparing meals, caring for younger children, and working to provide money for the family.

As illustrated in the stories related here, lower-class students are likely to have more obstacles to completing homework than middle- and upper-class students. Middle- and upper-class parents are more likely than lower-class parents to help with homework (Rothstein, 2004). When lower-class children are unable to complete homework because of family or economic conditions, teachers run the risk of unfairly punishing those children for factors beyond their control. Homework is most unfair when teachers fail to realize the limitations of the homework environment for lower-class students (Payne, 2008).

What if the way teachers use homework worsened the achievement gap between rich and poor students? Would that fact cause us to consider homework's use more carefully? When creating homework tasks, teachers should guard against assumptions about a child's home environment (Payne, 2008). When assigning homework, the following advice should be followed:

- Do not assume the child has a quiet place to do homework.
- Do not assume the child has a parent home in the evening.
- Do not assume the child's parents speak and read English.
- Do not assume the family has money for school supplies.
- Do not assume the child has access to materials such as paper, a pencil sharpener, scissors, glue, magazines, or a calculator.
- Do not assume the child has access to a computer or the Internet.

Teachers must remember that, regardless of social class, parents love their children and want the best for them. But most parents are not teachers, so they don't necessarily value homework in the same way that most teachers do. In discussing the fact that some families cannot afford supplies for homework projects, one teacher remarked, "They don't have money for posterboard, but they have money to buy $150 sneakers." That choice is not our call. How families choose to spend their money is a reflection of family values that may differ from our values. It is not our place to judge families based on *our* values.

If families cannot afford homework supplies, those supplies should be provided by the school. If money is not available in the school budget, funding should be pursued through the district, state grants, the PTA, local businesses, service organizations, or private donations from more fortunate parents (Huguelet, 2007). In the United States, a free public education is a right for all children. If we are public school educators, the assumption is that education is free, and children should not be required to purchase supplies for homework projects.

The Changing Parent-School Relationship

This discussion about values brings us to an important but delicate discussion about the parent-school relationship. As families have changed and become more democratic, their relationship with the school has changed as well.

To understand where we are, we must first reflect on where we have been. In previous generations, society was more authoritarian, and people were usually respectful of that authority. Workers usually obeyed their bosses, wives submitted to the authority of their husbands, and children submitted to the absolute authority of parents. Children were taught to address adults in their world as "sir" and "ma'am," and it was commonly accepted that children should respect their elders.

Schools, representing a sanctioned societal organization, maintained the status quo with absolute authority over children. Mothers were the primary contact for the school and, as women, were accustomed to being subservient to authority. In the authority hierarchy, teachers ruled over students and parents seldom questioned the authority of the school. Most parents endorsed the school's rules and accepted the judgment of teachers and principals. As many adults raised in the '50s and '60s remember, if you were in trouble at school, you were in trouble at home. Parents were a silent partner with the school, rarely entering into the decision-making process. When teachers asked for parental involvement, what they really meant was they wanted parents to help them reach the academic goals that they, as the educational experts, had deemed important. (Veteran teachers sometimes refer to these times as "the good old days.")

Parents assumed the school knew best. When children were assigned homework, parents dutifully obliged schools by making sure homework was done. For the many mothers who didn't work outside the home, taking responsibility for homework was less of a hardship than it is for many working parents today. Parents were willing partners in the homework practice. Although that scenario may still exist in some schools today, in many communities the relationship looks much different.

The Erosion of the Absolute Authority of the School

At some point in recent history, things began to change. As U.S. culture evolved to become a more democratic and more educated society, the parent's view of the absolute authority of the school began to change. Adults became less trustful of authority and, in general, less subservient to the authority of the school. Whereas in the past, parents had trusted that the school knew best, parents began to believe *they* knew something about education too. Teachers were no longer the only educational experts in the room. Teachers began to complain that "everyone's an expert on education just because they went to school." Many parents felt not only that school decisions *could be* challenged, but also that they *should be* challenged. Parents began to voice opinions about many decisions being made in the school—about discipline, schedules, vacations, dress codes, and the like. Noticing this change in parents caused one seasoned principal to say, "I prefer not to have parental involvement—it's more trouble than it's worth."

And so began the demise of the absolute authority of the school. Mirroring the death of the dictatorship in families discussed earlier, the school dictatorship began to die too. Many parents no longer viewed themselves as partners with teachers in the job of educating their child. They began to view themselves as clients for a service to be delivered. Instead of believing that they owed the school support, many parents began to feel that the school owed them a service. Coupled with this belief was the concept of parental freedom—that parents have the right to raise their children as they see fit.

A conspicuous example of this change in attitude is how parents today plan family vacations. Years ago, most parents would never have pulled their children out of school for a family trip, respecting the school's schedule and its strong discouragement of extended absences. Yet a 2006 survey showed that 61 percent of parents said they would take their children out of school for a family vacation, up from 45 percent in 2000 (Oyola, 2006). Many parents today believe they are entitled to remove their children from school for events *they* believe to be important, much to the chagrin of teachers and administrators. As one school principal acquiesced, "We have *so* lost that battle."

If this picture of parental support seems bleak, it is meant to be. It is meant to shock us into a reality check. Do all parents today feel that way about school? Of course not. But it is important to understand the perspective of those parents and to realize that the disconnect between the school's view and parents' views can be a major problem. We must be self-critical as educators and acknowledge that, in many schools, our relationship with parents has never been a partnership. Two moms expressed it this way:

> Few parents would call what we have with our kids' schools a "partnership" when we rarely have a say about our "part" or whether we want to turn our homes into second classrooms at night. Yet many of us feel we don't have a choice. (Bennett & Kallish, 2006, p. 58)

When teachers and principals complain that parents are no longer supportive of the school and teachers, they may be living in the past—when being *supportive* parents meant doing exactly what the teacher wanted, no questions asked. Those teachers and principals have failed to realize that a fundamental paradigm shift is occurring in the power relationship between parents and schools.

Respecting the Separate Power Structures of Home and School

Schools and families have always maintained separate power structures. For the most part, schools did not tell families how to raise their children, and parents did not tell schools how to teach their students. Parents maintained power over their children in the family, and teachers maintained power over children when they were at school. The school was expected to act *in loco parentis,* in place of the parent. Parents, in that sense, relinquished control of their children during the school day, when teachers acted in their place.

Schools have extended their reach into the family power structure in only a few areas, serving as an agent of the state to protect the best interest of the child. For instance, schools intervene to ensure that students attend school regularly and have had their immunizations. Schools are required by law to report abuse and neglect. Schools can prohibit sick children from attending school and can remove students who are a danger to others. But recently, when some schools began sending letters home to parents indicating their children were overweight, parents quickly protested that the school had unreasonably crossed the boundary between school and parental power structures. Increasing numbers of parents now believe homework has crossed that boundary as well (Bennett & Kallish, 2006; Kohn, 2006). Homework has become a contentious battleground in the fragile relationship between parents and school. As Goldberg (2007) puts it:

> Homework is an anomaly that transverses the boundary between family and school. It is a standard created at school for behavior to take place in the home. There is no other area in a child's life where an authority outside the parent has so much influence on policies and practices at home. . . . School . . . is mandatory, and homework has become an assumed extension of that legal mandate. (p. 4)

Goldberg goes on to explain that when homework works, parents aren't on the school's organizational chart at all. It's only when students fail to complete homework that the problem gets sticky, usually with lots of blaming on both sides. Consider if the following fable reflects any teacher or parent attitudes evident in your school.

A Fable

In EverySchool USA, as teachers began to assign more and more homework, they began to notice an erosion of parental support. Parents were no longer compliant about the homework teachers assigned. Parents now had their own agenda about what activities should fill their children's time outside of school. Parents were not sure homework should usurp their child's piano lessons, religion school, French lessons, or sports. Parents began writing notes asking that their child be excused from certain homework assignments. Along with an increasing diversity in parenting styles came an increasing diversity in the plans that parents had for their children's time outside school.

While parents felt entitled to control their child's free time, some teachers felt the parents were being downright uncooperative. "Shouldn't parents always support the school?" teachers asked. The teachers believed it was their obligation to extend learning beyond the classroom and that students and parents should comply. After all, they were only doing their job.

The principal and the teachers were still operating under the belief that they were totally in charge of the child's academic life. They believed they had the right to control the child's life outside of school for academic purposes. They were so sure of that right, they decided that parents were simply unaware of their parental responsibility and needed to be informed. So the teachers and the principal met and decided the way to fix the problem was to add a category on the student's report card that gave parents a "grade" for school support.

Well, that worked all right! The school support "grade" became the catalyst for a full-blown public relations disaster. Within a few days, parents were storming the office and tying up the phones with complaints. The local media got wind of the conflict, and the newspaper published an article with the headline "The Homework Blame Game at EverySchool." The principal learned the hard way about the disconnect between the teachers' and parents' beliefs. He learned the hard way that times had changed.

● ● ●

Renegotiating the Parent-School Relationship

The fable rings true in many ways. Some schools *are* out of touch with the needs of parents. Some parents *are* demanding more control over their child's homework schedule, and, yes, some schools *are* issuing report cards that give parents feedback on their "school support" (Jones, 2001). These may not be issues in your school. If parents are graciously compliant about homework and children dutifully complete homework with no negative effects, perhaps your school has no problem. But for those parents who have concerns, it will be necessary for teachers and principals to revise their expectations and renegotiate the relationship between school and parent. If the fable sounded familiar, it may be time to examine the parent-school relationship in your school.

Renegotiating the relationship will require teachers to compromise, respect parents' wishes, and relax a bit. One of our biggest handicaps as educators is our own anxiety about poor student performance and the belief that homework will save poorly performing students. Forging a true partnership for homework will require some hard work and some tough thinking. The following steps are a good start.

1. Get real. Homework critics bluntly state that schools should not be dictating what children do with their evenings (Kohn, 2006). Principals and teachers must accept that they are not totally in charge of a child's free time and that they do not have the right to demand that parents be involved with and support homework. That does not mean they must give up on homework completely—it just means they must be willing to compromise and respect the wishes of parents to control their child's time outside school.

2. Resist the temptation to judge. As teachers, it is easy to feel powerless when we need help, can't control parents, and feel overwhelmed. If we are teaching in a school with few resources, it is particularly frustrating. That frustration makes it tempting for teachers to judge—it's easy to blame both the parents and the student when homework is not completed. One teacher who was raised in poverty complained, "I did it. I was poor, but I knew it was my responsibility to do the homework, so I did it. If I did it, they can too." Perhaps she had supportive parents who strongly valued education, and perhaps she was blessed with drive and perseverance. Regardless of our own upbringing, this tendency to judge families from the perspective of the way *we* were raised is damaging to the parent-school relationship.

Sometimes it's easier to judge children as unmotivated or lazy than to reflect on our own teaching methods or to admit we don't have the tools, experience, or training to meet individual students' needs. But judging, blaming, and whining solve nothing. Teachers must accept the limitations of parental involvement and find ways to work with the support they have.

3. Revise expectations of parental support. A recent AP-AOL poll indicated a disparity between teacher and parent views of homework help. When parents were asked, "Thinking about the amount of time you spend helping your child with homework, do you feel it is usually too much, about right, or too little?" 57 percent of parents thought they were spending about the right amount of time. However, when teachers were asked, "In general, how would you rate the amount of time most parents spend helping their children with homework?" only 8 percent of teachers answered "about the right amount of time" and 87 percent of teachers answered "not enough time" (www.eschoolnews, 2006). This discrepancy might lead one to offer the following advice to teachers: When all else fails, lower your expectations!

What are reasonable expectations? Chapters 3 and 4 will discuss the specific types of tasks that are best for homework, but suffice it to say here that homework should not be used for new learning (Jackson, 2009). Parents should not be expected to teach their child a new skill. If the child has been given an assignment but has not yet acquired the skill, then the homework is inappropriate (Margolis, 2005). One 2nd grade parent was told by the teacher, "If you don't work with your daughter's penmanship, I'm going to have to send her to occupational therapy." When the parent asked at what point the child had failed to keep up with penmanship in class, the teacher responded, "We don't teach penmanship" (Bennett & Kalish, 2006, p. 74). In that situation, the teacher was asking the parent to teach a specific part of the curriculum, which is not the parent's role in homework.

Expectations are not demands. It is important to get parents' feedback about how much they want to be involved and to respect the wishes of individual parents. Schools should not expect that all parents will be involved with homework—that is the parent's choice.

4. Suggest (do not mandate) guidelines for the parent's role in homework. Most parents are unclear about what their role in homework is supposed to be. They often get different messages from different teachers as to what and how much they are supposed to do. They need more guidance and more communication from the teacher about expectations, but they also want teachers to respect what they as parents are willing and able to do in the homework process.

Parents should be encouraged to be *less involved* with the child's actual homework task and *more involved* in communicating with the teacher—writing notes when students don't complete work, asking for adaptations, or documenting how much time the child spent on the task. Parents should be encouraged to be observers, not enforcers (Goldberg, 2007).

If the child cannot do the homework without help, parents should be directed to stop the child and write a note to the teacher. If doing homework with their child is causing stress or conflict, parents should be directed to stop helping (Margolis, 2005). Parents should inform the school if they believe their child's homework load is excessive.

It is logical to expect parents to be somewhat more involved at the elementary level, less involved at the middle school level, and rarely involved at the high school level. During middle school, parents should be encouraged to wean their child off their homework help. Parents can be instructed to tell their children, "It's time for me to quit helping you with your homework" or "Mom's not taking algebra this year" (Vatterott, 2005). At the middle and high school levels, parents should back off tasks such as correcting mistakes, proofreading, or reviewing for tests. By this age, students should be self-checking and working with classmates to study or peer-edit. Homework advice for 7th and 8th grade parents should be "Don't touch it, don't pack it." At the middle and high school levels, teachers should work with students directly to make sure homework is completed and turned in. This assumes, of course, that school strategies are in place to prevent the student from failing as a result of incomplete homework (see the discussion of homework support programs in Chapter 5).

As schools attempt to define the parent's role in homework, they must realize that they can only *recommend* what parents should do. Given the new relationship between parents and schools, it would seem counterproductive for schools to *mandate* parental involvement in homework. Schools should work with their building's parent-teacher organization to come up with suggestions that clarify the parent's role in the homework process.

When designing homework guidelines for parents, wording is important. The phrases *parent guidelines* or *parent options* suggest a voluntary process, that parents have choices in what they will or will not do in regard to homework. *Parent expectations,* however, indicates that teachers *expect* parents to do certain things, meaning that if parents *don't* do those things, they—or their children—may be judged poorly. An example of suggested guidelines for the parent's role in homework is shown in Figure 2.1.

5. Establish formal methods of parent-teacher communication. A true partnership involves two-way communication that can be initiated by either party. Yet "researchers—and parents—report around 95 percent of school communication is one-way, with school officials telling parents what they or their children should be doing" (Jones, 2001, p. 21). Parents need guidance and specific tools to help them communicate with teachers about homework.

Figure 2.1	Suggested Guidelines for Parental Involvement in Homework

Parents are encouraged to . . .

Ask their child about what the child is studying in school.

Ask their child to show them any homework assignments.

Assist their child in organizing homework materials.

Help their child formulate a plan for completing homework.

Provide an appropriate space for their child to do homework.

Parents may, if they wish . . .

Help their child interpret assignment directions.

Proofread their child's work, pointing out errors.

Read aloud required reading to their child.

Give practice quizzes to their child to help prepare for tests.

Help their child brainstorm ideas for papers or projects.

Praise their child for completing homework.

Parents should not . . .

Attempt to teach their child concepts or skills the child is unfamiliar with.

Complete assignments for their child.

Allow their child to sacrifice sleep to complete homework.

A home schedule card (shown in Figure 2.2) allows parents or students to list their outside commitments. This can provide valuable information to teachers as they adapt assignments and deadlines to meet individual needs. A short parent survey such as the one shown in Figure 2.3 can help teachers understand parents' views about homework and their preferred level of involvement. (A longer version of the parent survey appears in the appendix.)

A parent feedback checklist (shown in Figure 2.4) can be used as a cover sheet for homework assignments. This checklist provides for two-way communication by allowing teachers to specify the amount of time a child should spend on an assignment and by giving parents options to check if the child is unable to finish

Figure 2.2	Home Schedule Card for Parents			

Child's name _____

Grade level _____

It would be helpful for your child's teacher to know how homework fits into your child's daily schedule. Please complete the homework card by writing down how your child typically spends time in the weekday hours when not in school (e.g., homework, sports practices, music lessons, visitation with noncustodial parents, dinner, sleep, play, TV, computer).

	Monday	Tuesday	Wednesday	Thursday
3:00–4:00 p.m.				
4:00–5:00 p.m.				
5:00–6:00 p.m.				
6:00–7:00 p.m.				
7:00–8:00 p.m.				
8:00–9:00 p.m.				
9:00–10:00 p.m.				
10:00–11:00 p.m.				

| Figure 2.3 | **Short Homework Survey for Parents** |

1. What grade is your child in? _____ What do you feel is an appropriate amount of homework for your child's grade level per evening?

2. How do you feel about weekend homework and homework over holiday vacations?

3. Who is in charge of homework? (Check all that you agree with.)

___ It is the parent's responsibility to make sure the child does homework.

___ Homework is the child's responsibility; parents should not get involved.

___ Parents have the right to excuse their child from homework without penalty for any reason.

___ Parents have the right to excuse their child from homework without penalty if it interferes with the child's sleep, health, or emotional well-being.

___ Parents have the right to excuse their child from homework without penalty if it conflicts with outside activities or family activities.

4. How much control should parents have over the amount and type of homework their child has? (Check all that you agree with.)

___ Parents should be able to request a limit on the *amount* of homework.

___ Parents should be able to request a limit on the *time spent* on homework.

___ Parents should be able to request *modifications* in the difficulty of assignments.

___ Parents should be able to request *additional* homework for their child.

___ The amount and type of homework is up to the teacher.

5. How involved are you with your child's homework? (Check all that apply to you.)

___ I don't get involved in my child's homework.

___ I check to see that my child's homework is done.

___ I have corrected my child's mistakes on homework.

___ I explain things that my child doesn't understand.

___ I help my child study for tests.

___ I have completed homework for my child just to get it done.

(continued)

Figure 2.3	Short Homework Survey for Parents (Continued)

___ I sometimes have trouble helping my child because I don't understand the directions.

___ I sometimes have trouble helping my child because I don't understand the material.

___ I'm not sure *how much* I should help my child with homework.

___ I have occasionally prohibited my child from doing homework because it interfered with sleep or family time.

Other_____

Figure 2.4	Parent Feedback Checklist

Dear Parent:

I estimate your child can complete this assignment in _____ minutes.

It is not necessary for your child to work longer than ____ minutes on this assignment, even if he or she does not finish it. Your child will not be penalized.

How much time did your child spend on this assignment?_____

If your child did not finish the assignment, please check the reason or reasons below:

___ My child could no longer focus on the task.

___ My child was too tired.

___ My child did not understand the assignment.

___ My child did not have the necessary materials to complete the assignment.

___ My child did not have enough time because of other outside activities.

___ Other reason (please explain). _____
_____
_____

_____
Parent signature

the assignment. A student version of the same checklist appears in Chapter 5.

6. Set parents' minds at ease about homework. An effective partnership also requires trust. Many parents have huge trust issues regarding teachers and homework, based on their past experience or the experiences of other parents. Some parents are afraid that talking to the teacher about homework will be ineffective or even harmful, which is understandable after hearing parent stories such as these:

> I've tried talking to my son's teacher about how he struggles with homework, but whatever I end up talking to her about, she uses it against my son the very next day and embarrasses him publicly. (From the mother of a 5th grader)

> At first I would write notes to the teacher telling her how my daughter wasn't able to finish because it was too much work. But my daughter would get benched at recess time. (From the mother of a 3rd grader)

A lot of anxiety has been created as such stories of teacher retribution are circulated among parents. Most teachers and administrators would be stunned by these stories, but unfortunately there are plenty of such stories to go around. Therefore, it is necessary for schools to establish ground rules so that parents feel comfortable talking to teachers about homework.

Again, school officials should work with parent groups to craft a schoolwide zero-tolerance policy stating that there will be no retribution, punishment, or embarrassment of students who do not complete homework. Also included in that policy should be a stipulation that students cannot be failed because of incomplete homework. (These ideas are discussed further in Chapter 4.)

7. Endorse a set of inalienable homework rights. As an additional sign of good faith, school leaders may wish to go one step further and adopt a set of homework rights for parents and children. Figure 2.5 is an example of a homework rights policy.

Figure 2.5	A Bill of Rights for Homework

1. Children shall not be required to work more than 40 hours a week, when class time is added to homework time.

2. Children shall have the right to homework they can complete without help. If they cannot complete homework without help, children shall be entitled to reteaching or modified assignments.

3. A child's academic grade shall not be put in jeopardy because of incomplete homework. Children shall be entitled to an in-school or after-school homework support program if they are unwilling or unable to complete homework at home.

4. A child's right to playtime, downtime, and adequate sleep shall not be infringed upon by homework.

5. Parents shall be entitled to excuse their child from homework that the child does not understand or is too tired to finish.

6. Families shall be entitled to weekends and holidays free from homework.

Summing Up

Because parents today are from different social and economic classes and have a variety of parenting styles and beliefs about the value of homework, traditional practices related to homework must be reexamined in light of that diversity. The power relationship between schools and parents must be realigned to embrace parents as equal partners in their child's education. The role of parents in homework must be voluntary, respectful, and individualized, and the value of family life must be honored.

3

Homework Research and Common Sense

What does the research say about homework, and how should we use that knowledge in making decisions about homework? As we examine the research on homework, it is important to understand the complexity of the process of homework, the limitations of the research, and the simplistic view of learning behind much of the research. Before using homework research to make educational decisions, it is important to first view the research through a critical lens.

A Complicated Practice

One would hope that the outcome of any instructional strategy, including homework, would be to improve learning. The problem is that homework involves the complex interaction of a number of factors (Cooper, 1989a; Corno, 1996). Educators know that differences exist in children, teachers, tasks, home environments, and measurements of learning, and that the interaction of homework and classroom learning is unique to individual students.

The whole game of homework is extremely complicated; homework is not necessarily a uniformly "good thing" for all students.

> Many if not most of teachers' purposes for assigning homework
> can only be accomplished under certain circumstances.... What
> is absolutely clear, from the bulk of the research evidence, is
> that the process of assigning and doing homework rarely works
> in the idealized way that laypeople—and apparently, most policy-
> makers—envision it. (Corno, 1996, p. 27)

When we try to relate homework to achievement, it is difficult to separate where the effect of classroom teaching ends and
the effect of homework begins. We don't know how to tease out the
effect of homework from prior learning or what occurred in the
classroom. We don't know if the same child would have scored
just as well on the test *without* doing the homework, or how much
better the child scored *because* of doing the homework.

Homework research is especially problematic because we're
attempting to study the effect of something that happens out of
our sight and out of our control. Unlike classroom learning, we
cannot be present when the homework is being done. We don't
know whether it was done alone, done with help from others, or
downloaded from the Internet. We can't watch it, we can't intervene
in the middle of it, and we're not even sure who did it! Because children differ and the conditions under which homework is completed
differ, researchers are, in a sense, drawing conclusions blind.

What Homework Researchers Choose to Study

Researchers choose to study and correlate specific factors about
the homework process. What they choose to study reflects mis-
perceptions about learning, a simplistic view of factors that
explain poor student performance—and therefore what factors
should be manipulated to improve academic achievement. Homework researchers often ignore student and teacher differences,
focus primarily on time, discount the home, and rely on tests as
the sole indicator of learning. Homework, like learning, is very
individual—yet researchers attempt to draw blanket conclusions,

reflecting the myopic view that all students learn the same thing in the same way.

The body of research on homework paints a curious yet familiar picture of traditional views of education. The research is predominantly about the following elements:

- *Time, not task* (reflecting the belief that more time is the answer to improving education)
- *Groups of students, not individuals* (reflecting a failure to recognize individual differences)
- *Student behavior, not teacher behavior* (reflecting the deficit model—that when children don't learn, the problem lies with them, not the quality of teaching)

Seldom do the studies factor in the role of good teaching or adaptations that teachers make for individual students. This picture is in sharp contrast to the current body of research about learning and the methods of more progressive educators—methods that reflect the importance of authentic and relevant learning tasks, the need to differentiate, and the belief that all children can learn once teaching methods are matched to their needs.

> Our current "scientific method" focuses almost exclusively on identifying what works best "generally" ... children differ. Therein lies what worries me about "evidence based" policy making in education. Good teaching, effective teaching, is not just about using whatever science says "usually" works best. It is all about finding out what works best for the individual child and the group of children in front of you. (Allington, 2005, p. 462)

General Findings of the Research on Homework

Do homework assignments improve achievement? The attempts of researchers to answer that basic question have led to conclusions that are inconsistent at best and contradictory at worst (Kohn, 2006; Trautwein & Koller, 2003). As noted by Cooper,

Conclusions of past reviewers of homework research show extraordinary variability. . . . Even in regard to specific areas of application such as within different subject areas, grades or student ability levels, the reviews often directly contradict one another. (in Buell, 2004, p. 10)

For almost every specific result shown, another study can be found that contradicts the result. Homework has generated enough research so that a study can be found to support almost any position, as long as conflicting studies are ignored. Both sides of the homework debate—pro-homework and anti-homework— can cite isolated studies that support their position (Cooper, 2007). Because the influences on homework are complex and subject to interpretation, scholars with opposing views have even used the same research to draw opposite conclusions! Almost any thesis about homework can be "proven" with statistics. Most of us remember little from our college statistics course, leaving us somewhat clueless as researchers attempt to prove their point with *effect sizes, stem and leaf tables,* and results deemed *statistically significant.* So when we read the following research findings, we must examine the evidence cautiously and view the results skeptically. The following are the major findings of the homework research.

Finding #1: The amount of time spent doing homework is positively correlated with achievement. Most of the homework research falls into one of two research designs. The first type, experimental or quasi-experimental, typically compares groups of students who received homework to groups of students who did not receive homework. Studies comparing students doing homework with students not doing homework showed that students doing homework had higher unit test scores than 73 percent of students not doing homework (Cooper, 2007).

The second type of design, represented by a large majority of the homework studies, examines the relationship between time spent on homework and achievement (Cooper, 2007). The majority of the studies found a positive correlation between time spent doing homework and achievement (Cooper, 2007). That is, as time spent on homework increases, achievement increases. Some studies, however, have shown a *negative* relationship between achievement and time spent on homework, meaning that *more time* spent was correlated with *lower* achievement.

Finding #2: Homework appears to be more effective for older students than younger students. Homework appears to be positively correlated with achievement, but the effect varies dramatically with grade level. In grades 3 to 5, the correlation was nearly zero; in grades 6 to 9, the correlation was .07; and in grades 10 to 12, the correlation was .25 (Cooper, 1989a; Cooper, Robinson, & Patall, 2006). Remember that 1.00 is a perfect correlation between two measures and zero means there is no correlation between two measures.

How is achievement measured in these studies? When studies correlate time spent on homework with achievement, achievement is usually measured by one of three types of data: scores on teacher-designed tests, grades given by teachers, or scores on standardized tests (Kohn, 2006). Cooper's meta-analysis of homework studies (Cooper, 1989b; Cooper et al., 1998; Cooper et al., 2006) combined studies with all three types of achievement measures to reach his cumulative correlations (described earlier) about time and achievement.

When those measures of achievement were viewed separately, Cooper and colleagues (2006) indicated that class grades (either general grades or grades on tests) showed slightly higher correlations with homework than did standardized tests, but that the difference in the two types of achievement was not significant.

Finding #3: As more variables are controlled for, the correlation between homework and achievement diminishes. Unfortunately, simply correlating time and achievement ignores many other variables that may affect achievement. The work of Keith and his colleagues is significant because they conducted research with large numbers of high school students. The discrepancy between their original research and their follow-up research is particularly revealing (see Cool & Keith, 1991; Keith, 1982; Keith & Cool, 1992). In their original research,

> Cool and Keith (1991) found a positive correlation between time spent on homework and achievement (r = +0.30). After controlling for motivation, ability, quality of instruction, course work quantity, and some background variables, however, no meaningful effect of homework on achievement remained. (Trautwein & Koller, 2003, p. 121)

So it appears that much of the correlation between time and achievement could be a result of the ability level of the student, the quality of instruction, or how rigorous the course was. Does homework cause higher achievement, or do high achievers spend more time on homework? Are higher-ability students more likely to take more challenging courses that require more homework?

Due to such discrepancies and other flaws in homework studies, researchers disagree as to whether homework enhances achievement. Whereas many hold strongly to their assertion that homework is beneficial (Cooper, 2007; Marzano & Pickering, 2007), others point to newer studies that seem to discount early research (Bennett & Kalish, 2006; Buell, 2004; Kohn, 2006). A new generation of homework studies using more sophisticated analyses "found no positive relationship between time spent on homework and achievement. Thus, most of the more recent results run counter to the results reported in Cooper's 1989 classic review" (Trautwein & Koller, 2003, p. 132).

Finding #4: At each grade level, there appears to be an optimum amount of homework. "There is no evidence that any amount of homework improves the academic performance of elementary school students" (Cooper, 1989a, p. 109). Does this mean there is no value in homework at the elementary level? Not necessarily. Several explanations for Cooper's conclusion are possible. First, younger students have less developed academic skills and shorter attention spans, and they require more adult assistance in learning, so working independently may be less productive. It is also possible that academic performance is difficult to measure at this age or that academic growth is slow and uneven. Even though the research cannot show a correlation, common sense suggests that time spent reading would improve reading skills, or that time spent practicing math facts would improve math skills. Perhaps this is why researchers, despite the data, often recommend that young children be given small amounts of homework.

For middle school students (grades 6 through 9), research shows that achievement improves slightly with even a minimal amount of homework (less than one hour). In other words, even a small amount of reinforcement of classroom learning seems beneficial. Achievement continues to improve until assignments last between one and two hours a night. Homework requiring more time than that is no longer associated with higher achievement (Cooper et al., 2006; Cooper, 2007).

For high school students (grades 10 through 12), achievement appears to improve until students are doing one-and-a-half to two-and-a-half hours of homework a night. At that point, achievement begins to decline (Cooper et al., 2006). "Correlational evidence suggests that high school students doing more than about two hours of homework a night achieve no better than those doing about two hours, and maybe worse" (Cooper, 2007, p. 37). The correlations with larger amounts of homework for middle and high school students seem logical, because older students are better able to work independently and for longer periods. One would hope that older students have also honed their study skills over the years.

The gist of the research, then, is that a small amount of homework may be good for learning, but too much homework can actually be bad for learning. This conclusion is what Cooper (2007) calls the "curvilinear relationship" between homework and achievement—that, up to a point, homework appears positive, but that past the optimum amount, achievement either remains flat or declines. Children as well as adults have a limit to how much mental work they can accomplish in a day's time before the brain needs downtime and time to process information (Jensen, 2000).

Curiously, the research about the appropriate amount of homework for different grade levels is consistent with an informal guideline that many teachers already practice. Both the National Education Association (NEA) and the Parent Teacher Association (PTA) have long endorsed what is called "the 10-minute rule" (origin unknown). The 10-minute rule states that the maximum amount of nightly homework should not exceed 10 minutes per grade level per night, all subjects combined. In other words, a 1st grader should have no more than 10 minutes of homework per night, a 6th grader no more than 60 minutes per night, and a 12th grader no more than 120 minutes per night. Those time limits are reflected in the curvilinear relationship Cooper noted—when the amount of time spent exceeds the 10-minute rule, that is the point at which a leveling out or decline in achievement is observed.

Limitations of the Research

The findings of the research on homework are limited by at least two important considerations: the overreliance on the work of one researcher and his colleagues, and individual differences among students.

Overreliance on Cooper's Work

Given the limited number of large-scale studies and the many smaller isolated studies that show conflicting results, it is difficult to draw reliable conclusions. As a result, we are forced to rely heavily on the work of one researcher and his colleagues—the only researchers to conduct any significant syntheses of the large number of studies. Dr. Harris Cooper of Duke University is widely regarded as the nation's leading researcher on homework.

Cooper, along with numerous colleagues, has conducted the most exhaustive reviews of the research (Kohn, 2006) and has published several compilations and meta-analyses of homework over the last 20 years (Cooper, 1989a, 1989b, 1994, 2001, 2007; Cooper et al., 2006; Cooper & Valentine, 2001). Although studies exist that are not included in his meta-analyses, his synthesis is probably the most useful for examining the research on homework. This situation leaves us in the dubious position of relying solely on one source of interpretation of the research—much like getting one's daily view of world events solely from one television network or newspaper.

As critical consumers, it is important to scrutinize not only Cooper's methodology but also the pervasive flaws in the homework research as a whole, which include the following:

- Many studies rely on self-reporting by students or parents as to how much time was spent on homework.
- Time spent on homework is measured as the cumulative time spent per week, not by the day.
- Sample sizes of students may be as small as a few students or a few classrooms.
- Often students are not randomly assigned to groups.
- Some studies measure homework assigned, not homework completed.
- Most studies lack equivalent control groups. (After all, what's an equivalent control group for a group of children when all children are different?) (Kohn, 2006; Trautwein & Koller, 2003)

Although Cooper's syntheses of homework research have been exhaustive, his reviews are uncritical. He simply combines the results of similar studies, performs statistical analyses, draws conclusions, and makes recommendations. At certain points after drawing conclusions, he may state a caveat relating to sample size or other factors, but his work is primarily statistical analysis, not a critique of the quality of the research (Cooper, 2007). In spite of this shortcoming, Cooper is the researcher most often cited when writers make recommendations about homework.

Aren't All Students Different?

In many of the research studies, groups of students are compared with each other (as when one class receives homework and another class does not). Regardless of attempts to randomize two groups of students, individual differences will still persist. Therefore, it is impossible to know what variations in achievement might be the result of differences in individual students as opposed to differences in the treatment, as noted by Trautwein and Koller (2003):

> Buell (2004) points out this fundamental problem with homework research: The research is conducted on subjects who are not uniform across time and space. . . . Homework may indeed "work" on one set of students but fail to work on another because of the varying sets of expectations and experiences brought to that homework. (p. 11)

A primary question that is seldom addressed is this: When achievement appears to be positively correlated with homework, is it due to the teacher or the student? Again, Trautwein and Koller (2003) comment:

> These large studies examine both class-level and student-level effects and claim that homework in general fosters achievement (class-level effect) *and* that students who spend more time on homework than do their classmates have better outcomes (student-level effect). However, these two possible effects are often mixed up. This is best exemplified by Keith and Page (1985). . . . In their study, "no homework is ever required" (teacher effect) and "I have homework, but I don't do it" (student effect) are collapsed into a single response category. (p. 122)

In fact, several different combinations of teacher effects and student effects could result in similar correlations of homework and achievement (Cooper & Valentine, 2001). Theoretically, effects at the student level and the class level could be opposite—one slightly negative and the other strongly positive—but when averaged together could yield an overall positive correlation with achievement (Trautwein & Koller, 2003).

A Commonsense Look at the Research

Taking a commonsense look at the research involves considering several aspects that may be problematic. These include the measures of time and achievement in the research, the assumptions made about cause and effect, and various caveats related to researcher bias, faulty conclusions, and questionable recommendations.

Common Sense About Time and Achievement

The measures of both time and achievement in the research are problematic. Just as educational reformers focus on extending the school day or the school year, homework researchers seem to be caught in the "seat time equals education" metaphor, as if more time is the answer. Remember that in most studies, time is measured as the cumulative amount of time spent per week, which tells us nothing about the frequency of the assignments (Trautwein, Koller, Schmitz, & Baumert, 2002). Remember, too, that measurements of time spent are usually self-reports by students.

Most studies don't consider that different students have different "working speeds" (Trautwein & Koller, 2003). More time spent on homework could indicate a slower working speed, or simply that those students complete all the homework assigned. Lumping together students who work at various speeds into one statistical profile renders the results questionable. When the research focuses on time instead of task, it fails to take into account which types of learning tasks contribute most significantly to learning.

Enlightened educators realized long ago that simply providing more time did not, by itself, produce more learning. Although time is a factor in learning, and engaged time is a necessity, children differ in the time they take to complete a learning task (Cooper, 2007). The learning that is accomplished is more important than how much time it takes. Learning is not a *Jeopardy!* game, in which people are judged by how fast they can access the answer, or an academic race where people are judged on how many facts they can recite in five minutes.

For individual learners, it makes sense that more time spent would equal more learning. Then why would some studies show that *more* time spent on homework is correlated with *lower* achievement? Those studies may be reflecting results for students with less prior knowledge or students with slower working speeds. When comparing slower processors to faster processors, the slower student could spend more time on homework and still perform poorly on tests (Cooper & Valentine, 2001).

Using teacher-made tests, grades, or standardized test scores to measure achievement is also problematic. Scores on standardized tests are least likely to be influenced by homework and are most likely to correlate with the affluence and educational level of parents (Kohn, 2000). Although teacher-made tests or grades may yield a correlation with homework, much research exists to refute the faulty logic that those measures actually indicate that learning has taken place (Guskey & Bailey, 2001; O'Connor, 2002). Teacher-made tests and grades reflect many things other than learning, such as the ability to memorize well, turn homework in on time, follow rules, and behave properly. Teachers are increasingly realizing the limitations of traditional tests to measure learning, causing many of them to move to performance-based assessments.

Common Sense About Cause and Effect: Correlation Is Not Causation

Just because high-achieving students do more homework does not mean that doing more homework *causes* higher achievement. It is just as likely that high-achieving students are good at homework and therefore do more of it. Yet many researchers attempt to infer causation when making recommendations based on their research. Alfie Kohn (2006) uses a colorful example to make this point:

> Statistical principles don't get much more basic than "correlation doesn't prove causation." The number of umbrellas brought to a workplace on a given morning will be highly correlated with the probability of precipitation in the afternoon, but the presence of the umbrellas didn't *make* it rain. . . . Nevertheless, most research purporting to show a positive effect of homework seems to be based on the assumption that when students who get (or do) more homework also score better on standardized tests, it follows that the higher scores were due to their having had more homework. (p. 28)

Beware of Researcher Bias

The conclusion of many researchers that homework *causes* higher achievement should be the equivalent of a large yellow caution sign reading "BEWARE OF RESEARCHER BIAS" or "*Proceed with caution: Results may be tainted by the researcher's inherent belief in the goodness of homework.*"

Conclusions of homework researchers cannot be divorced from their biases. Two people can do a meta-analysis and still draw two different conclusions due to their bias for or against homework. The homework research is rife with examples of conclusions not supported by the data and recommendations that go far beyond what is justified by the conclusions.

A good analogy is the researcher bias that is evident in medical research. For example, older studies of heart disease studied only men yet made blanket recommendations for heart health of both men and women. Studies touting the effectiveness of specific drugs have been questioned when it was discovered that the studies were financed by the company that manufactures the drug.

Beware of Conclusions That Don't Match Results

We must use research to inform yet have a healthy skepticism for what must naturally be a flawed process. Statistics being what they are, the same data can be extrapolated in different ways to present different and confusing results. Take, for instance, Cooper's data on the relationship between grade level and achievement. His research shows that the correlation of time spent on homework and achievement is higher at higher grade levels. In 2001, Cooper wrote this:

> For high school students (grades 10–12), a sizable average correlation was found (r = +.25), whereas for students in grades 6–9, the average correlation was small (r = +.07), and for elementary school students, it was nearly nonexistent (r = +.02). (p. 26)

In 2007, Cooper combined the data differently:

> We grouped correlations into those involving elementary students (grades kindergarten–6) and those involving secondary school students (grades 7–12). This was the best we could do given the precision of the data. The average correlation between time spent on homework and achievement was substantial for secondary school students, averaging about +.25 across 23 samples. For elementary school students, it hovered around zero for the average of 10 samples. (pp. 29–30)

This interpretation makes it appear that students in grades 7 through 9 benefited as much from homework as students in grades 10 through 12, a stark contrast to the earlier analysis that separated the data into the two groups.

Beware of Recommendations That Don't Match Conclusions

Just as we teach our students to be critical consumers of information and not to believe everything they read on the Internet, educators must be critical consumers of research as well. Research must always be examined carefully to determine its quality, its relevance, the logic of its conclusions, and whether the recommendations made are consistent with the conclusions of the study.

As mentioned earlier, Cooper (1989a) concluded that "there is no evidence that any amount of homework improves the academic performance of elementary school students" (p. 109). Marzano, Pickering, and Pollock (2001) cited that research as well. But the "innate goodness" of homework is so ingrained, researchers often don't see their own bias. Both Cooper and Marzano, after stating that the research shows no benefit of homework for elementary students, nonetheless proceed to recommend homework for elementary students. Cooper (2007) claims it should be given for the purpose of developing good study habits and positive attitudes (a recommendation not backed by any research). Marzano and his colleagues (2001) claim that some studies show that homework does produce beneficial results for young children, yet the studies they cite have been recently questioned by Kohn (2006). Marzano and his colleagues go on to conclude that because Cooper endorsed homework, students in 2nd grade and beyond should be asked to do *some* homework. Both researchers have such clearly ingrained biases toward homework that they don't appear to see the disconnect between the research they are citing and the recommendations they are making.

In fact, the pro-homework bias is so prevalent, researchers who find a *negative* correlation between homework and achievement often tend to discount their results:

> Researchers who report this counterintuitive finding generally take pains to explain that it "must not be interpreted as a causal pattern" . . . how rare it is to find these same cautions about the misleading nature of correlational results when those results suggest a *positive* relationship between homework and achievement. It's only when the outcome doesn't fit the expected pattern (and support the case for homework) that it's carefully explained away. (Kohn, 2006, pp. 29–30)

Should We Ignore the Research Altogether?

As we see the mismatches between research results and recommendations inherent in the homework research, we may wonder if there is any value in the research at all. Should we ignore the research altogether? No. Common sense tells us otherwise. The value of the research is in the broad strokes it paints, not in the minutiae. Its value comes as we reflect on the *logic* of its conclusions—do they make sense for *our* population of students? Are they consistent with what we have come to know from experience about our type and age of student? The other value of research is to dispel the myths behind some of the most strongly held beliefs about homework discussed in Chapter 1. We must remind ourselves that we're still not sure exactly how learning happens within different students and how much individuals differ in their learning needs.

Common Sense: 10 Things Teachers Know About Learning

Given the limitations of the research on homework, it would be easy to feel that we have no good compass to guide us in our use of homework. But that is not true—we have two very powerful bodies of knowledge that are germane to the decisions we make about homework.

First, much research exists about how children learn and the factors that influence learning. Research about the brain, time on task, motivation, persistence, and learner differences offer valuable insights into the design of homework tasks that support classroom learning.

Second, our own personal experience as teachers and administrators provides a wealth of information and perspective. Our experience has taught us much, especially if we have been reflective in our practice and have learned from others during our tenure. Experience has honed our common sense about teaching and learning. That common sense about education is really nothing more than our instincts and intuition about what works and what doesn't work. That common sense may be more valuable (and definitely more accessible) than all the research in the world. We can use what we already know from our own classroom experiences to guide our choices about homework (Buell, 2004).

In contrast to the widespread myths about homework discussed in Chapter 1, the truth is that several tenets about learning exist that directly affect the practice of homework in anyone's classroom. These tenets are explored briefly in this chapter and form the rationale for effective homework practices recommended in Chapters 4 and 5.

Tenet #1: Quality Teaching Matters

For the most part, the role of quality teaching in the effectiveness of homework has been ignored in the research (Wharton, 2001). Yet common sense tells us that classroom teaching must greatly influence homework. Homework is just one piece of the teaching-learning picture, one that is highly regulated by the teacher and, one would hope, connected to what happens in the classroom.

What if, instead of focusing on the student's homework behavior, we looked at the teacher's homework behavior? Have we considered the possibility that some teachers might use homework more *effectively,* might do more diagnosing and individualizing of homework? What if effective teachers provided more *appropriate* homework, homework that children might find worthwhile and enjoyable? One thing we know is that classroom organization, a teacher's homework habits, and attitudes and method of feedback all influence the effectiveness of homework. One group of researchers speculated about the connection between teacher behaviors and homework:

> Teachers who assign a lot of homework might differ from other teachers in nontrivial respects. Their lessons might be less organized, meaning that they have to assign more of the workload as

homework. Another difference may lie in their teaching styles: Teachers who assign a lot of homework may tend to assign the kind of homework that does not support learning in the best possible way. (Trautwein et al., 2002, p. 45)

Organization and structure of the learning process. How the teacher clarifies learning objectives, organizes content, scaffolds learning, and checks for understanding all contribute to the quality of learning for individual students. The general learning environment, whether orderly or chaotic, focused or distracting, may or may not be conducive to the effective use of homework.

• • •

Two 3rd Grade Classrooms

In Mrs. Sanders's 3rd grade classroom, the objective for the day's lesson is written on the board, as is tonight's homework assignment. She explains how to multiply two-digit numbers and does a sample problem. She checks for understanding by having students do two sample problems and check with their neighbors. She reminds students to write down the homework assignment and allows them a few minutes to do so, checking on certain students. She gives students 10 minutes to start their homework problems, during which time she walks around the room waiting for questions or confused looks. Zack is unsure about what he's doing. When Mrs. Sanders walks by his desk, he asks for help.

In another 3rd grade classroom, Mrs. Evans begins her lesson by explaining the purpose to the students, but some students are still assembling their materials and not listening. She shows students how to multiply two-digit numbers by doing two problems on the board. She does a third problem by asking the students what to do. A few students raise their hands to explain the steps, but not all students are engaged. She then orally tells students what the homework assignment is and tells them they have 10 minutes to begin their homework in class. Jason was not paying attention when Mrs. Evans gave the assignment and has asked another student what the assignment was. Melanie has trouble with oral instructions and also asks another student. Several students are talking softly to each other, which is distracting to some students who cannot concentrate on the homework. Andrew is confused but doesn't want to bother Mrs. Evans, who is now busy at her desk grading yesterday's homework assignments.

● ● ●

The teacher's homework behavior. The teacher's homework behavior relates to the quality and quantity of homework assigned, the discussing of homework in class, and the methods of checking or grading (Epstein & Van Voorhis, 2001). How homework supports a teacher's style of teaching and how much and how often homework is given will greatly affect whether homework is completed. Homework's connection to what happens in the classroom is also important. Is homework used in the classroom to inform lessons or is it unrelated? When teachers use homework to check for understanding, do they give nonpunitive feedback? Do they reteach concepts students did not understand? All of these teacher behaviors will affect how useful homework will be.

● ● ●

One Principal's Approach

At one elementary school, the principal refuses to allow her teachers to create six-week homework packets for students. At first glance, this decision was puzzling to the teachers. "Isn't it a good idea for students to have assignments in advance so they can work around their home and family schedules?" some asked. The principal explained, "Good teaching implies that teachers are constantly adjusting their teaching to the needs of the students. How do you know six weeks in advance which tasks students will have trouble learning, or which ones will require more time to learn? How do you know which tasks individual students will struggle with and who will need additional help?"

— • • • —

Teacher attitudes about homework. How teachers describe homework tasks to students and how they defend the purpose of homework say a lot about their attitudes. Is the purpose of the homework clearly connected to classroom learning, or is it just to be completed because the teacher said to do it? Is homework viewed as distasteful or used as punishment, or is a "no-homework pass" used as a reward for good behavior? Perception is everything, and students infer a lot from the attitude the teacher displays about homework. Those attitudes are usually revealed in the rewards and punishments doled out for completing or not completing homework on time.

How a teacher chooses to give feedback about homework can encourage or discourage a student from completing homework. (Feedback and grading are discussed in detail in Chapter 4.) Nonthreatening feedback with no grades attached provides positive information to students and keeps the focus on checking for understanding and learning. Detailed feedback is more effective than simple numbers or letters. When students receive no feedback on homework, it sends a message that homework is not important and not related to classroom learning. Overly harsh grading or late penalties increase student anxiety, and with older students such penalties often create a defiance to not do homework at all. One group of researchers speculated:

> The combination of a lot of homework and a lack of monitoring seems to indicate a rather ineffective teaching style with respect to learning. In other words, this interaction effect may reflect a generally inefficient teaching style rather than detrimental effects of homework on learning. (Trautwein et al., 2002, p. 43)

A teacher's comments and facial expressions in reaction to homework also send powerful messages. If a student does a homework assignment incorrectly, does the teacher blame the student for not paying attention or not working hard enough—"You must not have been listening when I explained it" or "Why did you do it this way?" (the student hears "What an idiot you are!"), or does he say something like "Oh, I guess my explanation didn't click—let's go over it again," reassuring the student that, in this classroom, it is safe to make mistakes?

Tenet #2: Skills Require Practice

Teachers know that certain learning skills require practice to perfect, and often homework is used for practice. Research confirms that mastering a skill requires focused practice (Marzano et al., 2001), but there are many conditions under which that practice may occur. First, we must make sure students are practicing the skill correctly, so they do not internalize incorrect methods (Trautwein & Koller, 2003).

● ● ●

Two Methods of Practice

Mr. Johnson demonstrates the steps in multiplying fractions and does two sample problems on the board. He then assigns 20 problems for homework practice. Susan correctly understood the steps and completes all 20 problems correctly. Sam, however, misunderstood and does all 20 problems incorrectly, practicing the incorrect way of multiplying fractions. Sam has great difficulty relearning the correct way later.

Mrs. Hernandez uses a different method. She demonstrates the steps and does sample problems. She then has everyone do problems in class and discuss what they did with their neighbor. She gives two-part math homework assignments. Part 1 asks students to explain the steps in the new process they have just learned and to do only three problems. (These she checks for understanding the next day.) Part 2 includes several practice problems of a process that students learned a few weeks ago. These are practice problems for a process she is sure they now understand and can do correctly.

• • •

Second, we must give students adequate time to practice before we assume they have internalized the skill correctly (Wright, 2006). Mrs. Hernandez's method (just described) is preferable because it allows for corrective feedback and the shaping of the skill that is practiced. Frequently teachers rush prematurely into a heavy practice phase, without adequately checking for understanding. A wiser approach would be to examine a few problems in depth and focus on the reasoning used to solve them before moving to the stage of practice (Marzano et al., 2001).

Third, an approach that uses smaller amounts of practice spread out over a number of days (distributed practice) is superior to an approach that uses larger amounts of practice done over a shorter period (mass practice). Shorter, more frequent periods of practice are better than longer assignments given less frequently (Trautwein et al., 2002).

Tenet #3: Time on Task Matters

Teachers know that more time on task helps learning and that homework is one way to gain more time for students to learn. We also know that some students need more time to process and internalize information. Suppose we tell all students to study for a test for 30 minutes. Will all students achieve the same results in 30 minutes? No—because there is a difference between the amount of time *spent on learning* and the amount of time *needed to learn*. Time *needed to learn* is influenced by aptitude, ability to understand instruction, and the quality of instruction (Trautwein & Koller, 2003). As many of us remember from our own experience as students, one student may study four times as long as another student, and both will earn the same grade on the test (Bryan & Burstein, 2004).

When all students are given a homework task of the same length, students who need more time to learn are at a disadvantage. An assignment that may take Amanda 30 minutes to complete may take Ben 90 minutes. If Ben is a high school student with homework in multiple subjects, he may need more time to learn than is available to him during nonschool hours. The dilemma then becomes how we provide those students with that extra time without overburdening them.

● ● ●

Homework Overload

Mrs. Devlin feels it is important to give lots of homework in her 9th grade U.S. History class, usually consisting of worksheets related to the book chapters. She feels she has so much content to cover that she cannot afford to take time in class to discuss the homework with students. She spends hours each night grading the worksheets and returns them to students without comment. She assumes it is their responsibility to learn from the textbook on their own, and her lectures cover material that is not covered in the textbook. Several students are failing because they cannot complete the large amount of homework required.

● ● ●

For students who need more time to learn, teachers will find it necessary to prioritize work or limit the number of standards that individual students are expected to master (Margolis, 2005). This is a common practice for special education students, but it may be necessary for other students as well. By prioritizing homework in specific subjects and reducing the length of homework assignments, it is possible to give students adequate time to learn.

(More options for extending the amount of time students have for homework are discussed in Chapter 5.)

Time on task refers to teachers too. They need adequate time to plan effective classroom activities. What if more time spent grading homework equaled less time to plan quality classroom instruction, which could affect the quality and amount of learning that occurs in the classroom?

Tenet #4: Task Is as Important as Time

The quality of the homework task is as important as the amount of time required (Bryan & Burstein, 2004). Students make decisions about whether to attempt homework based on their assessment of the task. Is the homework perceived to be interesting or boring, simple or tedious? Students are less likely to complete tasks they perceive as busywork. Quality homework tasks allow students to practice or process information, introduce them to material that will be discussed in the future, or provide feedback to teachers so they may check for understanding. Quality tasks are clearly related to classroom learning, are simple enough that students can complete them without help, and, it is hoped, are relevant to real life. (Examples of quality homework tasks are presented in greater detail in Chapter 4.)

Tenet #5: Learning Is Individual

Teachers know that each student is unique and that each student learns differently. A basic concern about the homework research is that it reports on *averages*. The 10-minute rule, for instance, suggests that 10 minutes of homework per grade level per night is the maximum amount of work that should be assigned. But that is an *average*—which means that for some students, the optimum amount of homework will differ. For instance, some 6th graders may be capable of sustaining attention and benefiting from 60 minutes a night, some may be capable of working 90 minutes a night, and others may have trouble completing just 30 minutes of homework and may not benefit from more.

Because learning is individual, some students learn quickly in the classroom and may not require any practice or reinforcement—but others will. In any case, each student will have an optimum amount of time that he or she can work effectively on homework. Some students will need shorter assignments, and some assignments will need to be prioritized for mastery.

●　●　●

No Homework Necessary?

Patrick is a very bright 10th grader taking chemistry, biology, and the highest-level math courses his school offers. He learns math quite easily, never does homework, and still makes As on all the tests. Luckily his science teacher, Mr. Richardson, does not count homework in Patrick's grade. Other teachers believe that Mr. Richardson is wrong not to require Patrick to do the homework.

●　●　●

Homework needs to be personalized to fit the specific needs of individual students. Some students will have less time available, some students will have less supervision, and some students will need more sleep or downtime than other students. (Methods for individualizing homework are discussed in Chapter 4.)

Tenet #6: Children Differ in Readiness and Developmental Level

Whether they are in elementary, middle, or high school, students differ in their level of previous knowledge, the sophistication of their academic skills, and their readiness for new learning (Wright, 2006). New learning must be scaffolded onto existing frameworks (Buell, 2004). Students with limited readiness may need more direct instruction, practice, concrete experience, or simpler reading material (Allington, 2002; Margolis, 2005). More advanced students may benefit from tasks that are more challenging or the opportunity to explore topics in greater depth (Tomlinson, 2003; Vatterott, 2007).

Diagnosis of individual students' levels of readiness is an important job for teachers (Bryan & Burstein, 2004). Homework can initially be used for diagnosis and then can be adapted to fit individual student needs. "For a teacher, understanding a student's level of development is crucial, as is spotting where, when, and why mistakes are made in learning something new" (Buell, 2004, p. 18).

Common sense tells us that differentiated instruction is necessary and desirable, yet when it comes to homework, teachers often assign the same task to all students, regardless of their level of readiness (Bryan & Burstein, 2004). (Chapter 4 discusses how homework tasks should be differentiated to meet individual student needs.)

Tenet #7: Children Differ in Learning Style

Research on learning styles, multiple intelligences, and the brain has shown that students have a profile for the way they learn best (Dunn & Dunn, 1978; Keefe & Jenkins, 2002). Learners' preferences may be auditory, visual, tactile, or kinesthetic. Some may require diagrams or schematics, whereas others may learn easily through reading. Some may prefer tasks that allow them to use drawing, music, or bodily movement to express what they have learned or to help them remember factual information. Numerous studies have found that student achievement increases when teaching methods match students' learning styles (Gardner, 1999; Vatterott, 2007). Yet teachers often fail to adapt homework for individual learning styles. By providing choices and flexibility in homework tasks, teachers can accommodate differences in learners and therefore increase the effectiveness of homework (Bryan & Burstein, 2004; Vatterott, 2007).

• • •

Homework Geared to Individual Learning Styles

Miss Lee knew it was important for her 4th graders to know their multiplication tables by memory. The students' homework assignment was to design a method to help them memorize their multiplication tables. She gave them several suggestions, such as writing them, reciting them, or making charts. The students were free to design whatever method they thought would work best for them. Some of the students' methods included writing a rap song, using pictures, making a poster with rows of stickers, and making their own flash cards. Each student was then required to log how much time he or she spent practicing each week. Students shared their methods with other students in the class and were allowed to practice with each other's methods.

• • •

Tenet #8: Children Differ in Motivation, Persistence, and Organizational Skills

Homework is a classic form of self-regulated learning. Students decide whether, when, and how to tackle the homework tasks they have been assigned (Trautwein & Koller, 2003). Children differ in their level of motivation, and that motivation to complete homework is mediated by several factors.

First, students who have a feeling of competence about learning are more likely to do homework. The feeling of competence is influenced by a student's expectation of success, which is based on past experience (Trautwein & Koller, 2003). Therefore, students who have an academic history of doing poorly on homework assignments need tasks at which they can be successful. They need positive feedback for completing homework—positive experiences to "undo" the negative experiences of the past (Sagor, 2008).

Second, completing homework requires perseverance. Students with a positive self-concept or self-efficacy are more likely to persist when faced with difficult tasks (Sagor, 2008; Trautwein

& Koller, 2003). Students who lack perseverance may lack strategies. They may ask, "What should I do when I don't understand the assignment?" Students who lack strategies may not think to look back over what they have read or to call a friend for help (Bryan & Burstein, 2004). They may lack metacognitive skills such as orienting, planning, executing, monitoring, evaluating, and correcting (Levine, 2003). A lack of metacognitive skills often leads to students abandoning tasks too easily (Garner, 2008). Some students, especially students with special needs, give up on tasks rather quickly, having developed "learned helplessness," which is often unwittingly reinforced by family members. Families that supervise homework and value persistence may encourage students to keep working, while other families may not. Motivation and persistence are also influenced by student interests and the value the student attaches to the task (Margolis, 2005). Wise teachers seek feedback from students and consider how they might tap into student interests.

* * *

Adapting to Students' Needs

Mrs. Turner quickly realized that handwriting was hard for many of her 5th graders, especially her special education students, who wrote more slowly. She allowed some students to do many of their homework assignments by typing. She discovered that when she gave students that option, the number of missing and incomplete assignments decreased.

Mr. Carr insisted that all homework for his 5th graders be handwritten. He believed that this was one way to ensure that students would not cheat and that it would give students additional practice at handwriting. However, he frequently complained that students' papers were sloppy and sometimes illegible. Some of his students who struggled with handwriting often turned in incomplete homework or failed to turn in work at all.

* * *

Tenet #9: Frustration Is Detrimental to Motivation and Desire to Learn

Some teachers will say that frustration in learning is good and necessary. For the achievement-oriented student who has successfully overcome frustration in the past, that may be true. These students may have a higher tolerance for frustration and therefore be motivated to try harder. But for students who are fearful of failing and being judged, frustration is a cost they may not be willing to pay, especially if they possess no strategies for getting beyond the frustration. Differences in motivation, persistence, and organizational skills oblige teachers to adapt homework assignments to provide opportunities for maximum success and minimum frustration for each student. This obligation means homework assignments should be time based—students should be instructed to do as much as they can in a certain number of minutes and given feedback on what they complete. Students who have trouble persisting with difficult tasks must be given work that is doable and must be provided one-on-one assistance (Darling-Hammond & Ifill-Lynch, 2006). Their homework should be monitored more closely, with an emphasis on progress and with improvement noted and praised (Wright, 2006). They must be taught concrete strategies, assigned study buddies, or provided after-school support programs. (All these remedies are discussed in Chapters 4 and 5.) For students who have difficulty persisting with homework, checking for frustration is as critical as checking for understanding.

● ● ●

Checking for Frustration

Mrs. Johnson asks her 2nd graders to write the number of minutes they spent on each homework assignment at the top of the page. She also has three circle faces at the top of the assignment—one smiling, one neutral, one frowning. Students circle a face to describe whether they thought the assignment was very easy, doable, or very hard. Mrs. Johnson uses this feedback to check for learner frustration and to adjust the difficulty of assignments for specific students.

• • •

Tenet #10: Homework That Is Not Completed Doesn't Help Learning

We know that if homework is not completed, it doesn't help anything. Assigning homework does no good if students don't do it. On the other hand, well-designed homework that students complete successfully can reinforce classroom learning and allow for additional time on task.

Summing Up

The homework research is a cautionary tale, not a hard-and-fast prescription for action. We want to know what the research says, but it is not prudent to be a slave to the numbers. The inability of research to prove homework's usefulness does not mean that homework *cannot* be useful or worthwhile; it just shows that homework *has not* been useful in many cases. The research does not validate the love affair some teachers seem to have with homework. If we choose to give homework, how should we give it? Very carefully. We should reflect carefully about its purpose, plan the nature of the task carefully, and assess homework carefully to check for understanding.

Our own classroom experience provides much common sense about how to coordinate classroom learning and homework in a way that uses homework effectively. Many experienced teachers would maintain that teaching is more art than science, and although the science of research may inform our actions, it must not dictate them. The needs of individual learners must be the driving force behind all instructional decisions. Children are not seeds in a petri dish or rats in a maze. They are dynamic, thinking, feeling human beings, each with unique learning needs. Learning is a complex process that, despite all our research, we still struggle to understand. Chapter 4 discusses how to create quality homework tasks that will support classroom learning for individual students.

4

Effective Homework Practices

Chapters 4 and 5 bring us to the question most teachers want answered: "How can I get them to do their homework?" (Darling-Hammond & Ifill-Lynch, 2006). We often tend to look for the quick fix—expressing concern more about "How can we *make* them do their homework?" instead of looking more deeply at "Why *don't* they do their homework?" The search for answers is a complex one that requires us to conduct a methodical examination. Many strategies exist to improve the rate of homework completion, but before discussing those strategies, we must rethink how common practices may contribute to the problem. We must look at the old paradigm of how we *do* homework and suggest a new paradigm.

Rethinking Common Homework Practices: The Old Paradigm

The old homework paradigm is a set of common practices driven by the traditional beliefs and attitudes that were discussed in Chapter 1. The paradigm is built upon such ideas as the belief in the inherent goodness of homework, the assumption that the homework is doable and any problems are related to motivation, the belief that the key to controlling student behavior lies in reward and punishment, and the attitude that homework should be completed simply because the teacher told the student to do it.

Chapter 3 revealed what common sense and experience tell us about learners. Despite what teachers know from experience about learners and learning, when it comes to homework, common sense is often not reflected in common practice. For instance, we know that students differ in their readiness and developmental level and that all students do not learn in the same way, yet homework is often one-size-fits-all, with all students being assigned the same task (Eisner, 2003–2004).

We know that students differ in their "working speed"—that some take longer to learn a concept or complete tasks than others—yet teachers often expect slower students to take the additional time to complete the same homework task that other students finish more quickly. The remedy often is to give the child *more time* instead of *less work* (Goldberg, 2007). Homework completion is often task based, regardless of how long it takes individual learners to do a particular assignment.

We know that students have responsibilities and activities outside of school, yet homework is often assigned at 3:00 p.m. one day and expected back the next day. We know that families differ in their priorities, yet many teachers believe all students should arrange their daily schedules to put homework first. These common practices reflect the old paradigm—how we *do* homework.

The beliefs and assumptions inherent in the old paradigm, coupled with the history of behaviorist practices in education, create a strange dynamic: when students fail to complete homework, we tend to approach the situation more like discipline than like learning. That is, remedies for students who don't do their homework tend to focus on punitive solutions as the key to changing behavior—consequences such as points off, failing grades, or missing recess or lunch to complete homework. We tend to get stuck in the reward/punishment box. Yet somehow, in our hearts, we know that we cannot *punish* students into completing homework.

Grading in the Old Paradigm

A primary method of reward and punishment for homework is grading. In fact, grading plays a huge role in the old homework paradigm. In an effort to force compliance, teachers give zeros for incomplete homework, and late policies mandate points off for each day homework is turned in late. Depending on what percentage homework counts for in the student's total grade, many *D*s and *F*s can result each semester from incomplete homework. The question arises: What do those *D*s and *F*s represent—a lack of learning or a lack of compliance?

Teachers often defend late policies by saying they are using them to teach responsibility. As discussed in Chapter 1, the teaching of responsibility is a much-touted goal, conjuring up images of compliant children dutifully toiling over whatever task was assigned to them (Kohn, 2006). Homework can play an important role in the development of that self-direction. However, those skills are not developed simply by assigning homework tasks and applying consequences if tasks are not completed (Kohn, 2006). The flaw in this concept lies in the implementation—when students don't complete homework on time, late policies punish them for *not learning* responsibility! So if they don't complete homework on time, doesn't that mean that the teacher has failed to *teach* them responsibility? If that is true, the logical act would be to *reteach* them without penalty. Instead, the use of late policies judges students for not learning responsibility and then fails them as a result.

What if all the students in our class failed to turn in homework on time? Would we fail everyone? Or do we only penalize some students for incomplete homework because we can compare the "good" students to the "bad" ones? Do late policies allow us to norm-reference our grades—and achieve a bell-shaped curve?

• • •

Homework 40, Football 0

In a high school in Texas, homework counted for up to 40 percent of the student's grade, depending on the subject. One year, even with tutoring from their coach, many members of the junior varsity football team were not keeping up with homework and were failing to make the minimum grades required to play sports. Primarily as a result of homework, the junior varsity football season had to be canceled one year.

Does this seem like a reasonable consequence? How would you prevent this situation from happening in the future?

As a solution to the problem, teachers decided to give less homework but make it count more in the grade. (Huh?)

• • •

As discussed in Chapter 2, when we use grades to punish late homework, we are often penalizing students for their home environment. It's not fair if students are punished because they have not had the opportunity to do the homework while at home. One student told her teacher, "My mother won't let me do homework." When questioned further, the student explained that she was required to cook, clean, and take care of younger siblings from the time she got home from school until bedtime. (Chapter 5 discusses a variety of solutions to this problem, other than failing grades.)

Although teachers often agree it is not fair to fail students because of homework, invariably someone will ask, "What about the less able student who actually passes *because* he or she has turned in homework?" That brings us to another grading dilemma. Homework should not cause children to fail, but should homework alone allow students to pass? Even if homework tasks reflect learning, it is difficult to be sure the student was the person who did the work. (Have you seen some incredible science fair projects from children of engineers?) Learning can be validly assessed only in the classroom or through external projects that have been closely monitored. Effort on homework alone should not equal a higher grade if the student cannot demonstrate knowledge of the content while in the classroom (Guskey, 2003). Rewarding effort in the absence of learning is not a problem except when the reward is a grade, which is supposed to reflect learning. By allowing students to pass based on homework, we are still using grades to manipulate behavior, again rewarding compliance and not necessarily learning.

Rewarding homework compliance with good grades can backfire when those grades do not reflect learning. In one school where homework counts heavily in student grades, the principal tells the story of a 7th grade girl who had received straight As on her report card but whose parents were upset that she tested at a 4th grade reading level. Similarly, high school teachers have witnessed students with very high grades due to homework who could not earn decent scores on college entrance exams.

Limitations of the Old Paradigm: Why It Doesn't Work

Inherent in the old paradigm are the assumptions that all students can do the work (not all of them can), that all students have the time to do the work (not all of them do), and that students should take as much time as is necessary to do the work (not all of them will). The old paradigm "operates on the implicit notion that the child is capable of doing the work" (Goldberg, 2007, p. 15). When students are given homework that is beyond their comprehension level or that is too lengthy and are then penalized with failing grades for incorrect work, the experience is frustrating and demotivating (Past, 2006; Vatterott, 2003). When those grades are permanent, there is no redemption for mistakes. Homework can also do harm when a student misunderstands a concept or a process (such as the steps in solving an equation) and homework causes the student to reinforce misconceptions or internalize bad habits.

For students who *can* do the homework and complete assignments on time, grading can be a positive experience. But for those students who struggle, the old homework paradigm leads to what Goldberg (2007) calls the "homework trap":

> Late work means points off, and work not done garners zeros. Their grades decline, setting into motion a number of actions by the parents and the school, with counteractions (usually inactions) by the children themselves. The problem is cumulative and colors the experiences these children have with school, affecting their attitudes and performance in later years. (p. 1)

After a while, failing grades from incomplete homework accumulate and are almost impossible to counteract. This can lead to a feeling of helplessness—why bother to even try to catch up? The homework trap activates the following chain reaction:

> Incomplete homework→poor grades→poor attitudes→a predictable avoidance of homework and a resentment toward the system→more failing grades. (adapted from Goldberg, 2007, p. 2)

What the homework trap shows us is the importance of the emotional dynamic of the assessment experience (Stiggins, 2007). Motivation and a sense of competence are key factors in student success. Because grading is perceived by students as judging, it separates students into winners and losers. It is precisely the practice of punishing noncompliance regarding homework that interferes with the effective practice of homework, to the detriment of learning and motivation.

The goal of assessment of learning should be to keep failure at bay and to maintain the learner's confidence—the opposite of what occurs in the homework trap. The most important question to ask about the grading of homework is "What is the effect on future learning?" (Stiggins, 2007). Priority must be given to tasks that do not cause students to give up.

What is the result of not being a successful player in the homework game? Motivation to learn may be affected as well as learner identity. Students on a "losing streak" feel hopeless. They begin to think, "This hurts. I'm not safe here; I just can't do this . . . again. I'm confused. I don't like this—help! Nothing I try seems to work" (Stiggins, 2007, p. 24). In such situations, homework can actually discourage some students from further learning. To protect their self-esteem and reputation, these students often adopt a cover; they claim they don't do homework because they "just don't want to" rather than admitting they don't understand the assignment or don't have the time or the proper conditions to do homework (Olson, 2008).

Luis's Story

Luis was failing social studies because he was missing 11 assignments. When the teacher's aide tried to find out why, Luis said, "I'm lazy." In fact, Luis felt hopelessly buried in work. The teacher's aide volunteered to stay after school to help Luis catch up. It was hard convincing Luis to stay after school, but after several work sessions, he was caught up and no longer called himself lazy.

The homework trap explains why some students don't do homework. The trap shows how we set them up for failure and why they give up. Often, the result is students who simply refuse to do homework. The old paradigm gives students that option—students who do not complete homework are given failing grades but are not required to complete the work. Not only does this cause students to receive failing grades, but it also puts some students at a disadvantage. If the homework they are not doing is quality homework, a gap in skills and confidence may arise between students who regularly complete homework and those who do not, often exacerbating the achievement gap.

Simply stated, the old paradigm short-circuits our long-term goals by allowing students to fail by not doing homework. It creates practical and motivational obstacles that converge to form the perfect storm for student failure. Traditional practices can actually discourage the very quality we are trying to instill: accountability. "We are faced with the irony that a policy that may be grounded in the belief of holding students accountable (giving zeros) actually allows some students to escape accountability for learning" (O'Connor, 2007, p. 86).

The old paradigm was about compliance with authority, but today our long-term goals go beyond compliance. Our long-term goals are for students to have self-discipline, to perfect their intellectual skills, and to feel confident as learners. When some students don't do homework (quality homework, that is), they can find themselves at a disadvantage. A homework gap can emerge between those students who regularly complete homework and those who do not. The homework gap can compound the problem of the achievement gap that already exists between children of different social classes and can impede the long-term goals we have for all students.

What we want is to develop and refine intellectual skills—but when students don't do homework, they may not perfect math skills, may not read as well, or may lack depth of knowledge for future learning. Quality homework tasks can play an important role in the development of those skills and the acquisition of that knowledge. When students fail to complete quality homework on a regular basis, it can mean less time spent learning content and skills—less time to process content, less time to perfect skills. Students may fail to develop an in-depth understanding of concepts or may not read as well as they should. Skills that require practice, such as math skills, may not be perfected, thus handicapping the student for higher levels of learning. For some students, the result may be a shaky foundation of content knowledge and skills and less cumulative learning, both of which can hinder future learning endeavors. This diminished cumulative learning can also weaken the student's performance on standardized tests such as the ACT or the SAT, where lower scores can limit the student's access to college.

The effect of homework grades may also be negative. First, if incomplete homework produces poor results on course assessments, lower grades may result. Second, when incomplete homework is counted as a zero in the total average, students receive lower grades for the semester or the year. In some cases, these lower grades may cause students to fail subjects in elementary school or courses in middle school or high school. At the elementary and middle school levels, failure in more than one subject may be grounds for retention. For high school students, failing semester grades affect grade point average, which again influences their access to college.

What we want is to develop independent learners—but when students don't do homework, they may fail to develop strategies for independent work and may miss the sense of efficacy that comes from completing tasks independently. In addition to the negative effect of failing grades, students who fail to complete homework may miss the opportunity to experience success as an independent learner. The result is a decrease in motivation and learner self-esteem, which influences the student's desire to continue formal learning. This combination of failing grades and lack of successful learning contributes to students' disengagement from school and further disenfranchises them from the school community.

What we want is to nurture within students the identity of a successful learner—but when students don't do homework, they may have trouble keeping up in class, may receive failing grades, and may lose confidence in their ability to learn. The student who regularly completes homework is most likely prepared for class, has studied for tests, and may be viewed by the teacher as a compliant, hard-working, serious student. The student who does not complete homework may be unable to understand or follow classroom lessons, may be unable to participate in class, and may be viewed as a less-than-serious student. Students who do not complete homework may be viewed as unmotivated by teachers and other students and may even develop a reputation of being lazy.

Getting Homework Right: Creating a New Paradigm for Homework

To reach our long-term goals as well as to meet short-term academic purposes, it is necessary to create a new homework paradigm that focuses on academic success for all students. Creating such a paradigm requires a comprehensive set of practices that can improve academic success when implemented as a package. Those practices are the following:

- Designing quality homework tasks
- Differentiating homework tasks
- Moving from grading to checking
- Decriminalizing the grading of homework
- Using completion strategies
- Establishing homework support programs

Before addressing the first of these (designing quality homework tasks), we must consider the purpose of the homework task—how it relates to what is learned in the classroom—and what type of learning is desired.

What Is the Purpose of the Homework Task?

Homework typically supports learning in one of four ways: prelearning, checking for understanding, practice, or processing.

Prelearning. Homework may be used to provide an introduction to a topic or background for a more in-depth lesson (such as reading or outlining a chapter before a discussion). Prelearning may be as simple as finding out what students already know about a topic or what they are interested in learning about (such as asking them to write down questions they have about the digestive system). Prelearning may also be used to stimulate interest in the concept (such as listing eye color and hair color of relatives for a genetics lesson).

Checking for understanding. Checking for understanding is the most neglected use of homework, yet it is the most valuable way for teachers to gain insight into student learning. For instance, asking students to do a few sample problems in math and to explain the steps lets the teacher know if the student understands how to do the problem. Journal questions about a science experiment may ask the student to explain what happened and why. Asking students to identify literary devices in a short story shows the teacher whether the student understands literary devices.

Practice. The traditional use of homework has been for the practice of rote skills, such as multiplication tables, or things that need to be memorized, such as spelling words. Although practice is necessary for many rote skills, there are three mistakes that teachers sometimes make with the use of practice homework. First, teachers may believe they are giving practice homework when, in fact, the student did not understand the concept or skill in class. The homework then actually involves new learning and is often quite frustrating. Second, if teachers skip the step of checking for understanding, students may be practicing something incorrectly and internalizing misconceptions. For instance, students should practice math operations only *after* the teacher has adequately checked for understanding. Third, distributed practice is better than mass practice—that is, practice is more effective when distributed over several days (Marzano et al., 2001). In other words, a student may need to practice a math operation 50 times to master it, but not all in one night! A common practice for math teachers today is to give two-tiered math homework: for example, Part One is 3 problems to check for understanding of a new concept, and Part Two is 10 problems to practice a concept previously learned.

Processing. Processing homework is used when we want students to reflect on concepts that were discussed in class, think of new questions to ask, apply skills or knowledge learned, synthesize information, or show that they see the big picture. Processing homework is often a long-term project, such as summarizing major concepts in a unit, writing an original poem, or applying a number of math concepts to the design of a golf course.

What Type of Learning Is Desired?

When planning homework tasks, teachers should also reflect on the type of learning they want the homework to reinforce. Classroom learning may be composed of one of five types of learning:

- *Facts*—Discrete bits of information that we believe to be true (e.g., whales are mammals)
- *Concepts*—Categories of things with common elements that help us organize, retain, and use information (e.g., the process of photosynthesis)
- *Principles*—Rules that govern concepts (e.g., matter can change forms)
- *Attitudes*—Degrees of commitment to ideas and spheres of learning (e.g., we should be concerned about the environment)
- *Skills*—The capacity to put to work the understandings we have gained (e.g., drawing conclusions from data) (adapted from Tomlinson, 1999, pp. 38–39)

The *type of learning* that is desired and *the purpose of the homework* determine the *type of homework task* the teacher should design. This relationship is illustrated in Figure 4.1.

Understanding the purpose and type of homework will not, by itself, ensure that students will be motivated to complete homework tasks. Although motivation is complex and unique to individuals, teachers can increase the likelihood that homework will be completed by considering the needs of the individual learner in the design of the homework task itself.

Figure 4.1	Relationship Between Classroom Learning and Homework Tasks		
Type of Learning	**Purpose of Homework**	**Example of Skill or Content**	**Example of Homework Task**
Facts and concepts	Prelearning	Main ideas of chapter	Complete an advance organizer of the chapter.
Facts and concepts	Prelearning	Vocabulary words and definitions	Draw pictures to illustrate each vocabulary word.
Skill	Checking for understanding	Reading comprehension	Create a concept map of the chapter.
Skill	Checking for understanding	Division of fractions	Explain the steps; do three problems.
Skill	Practice of skill	Division of fractions	Do 10 practice problems and write 2 word problems for other students to solve.
Facts	Practice of rote memory	Multiplication tables	Write, recite, or create a grid of multiplication tables.
Concept	Processing—to study for test	Chapter 5—The Colonial Period	For each section, answer these questions: What do I know about this section? What do I still need to study?
Concepts/ principles	Processing— analysis and reflection	Boston Tea Party	Write an editorial defending or criticizing the actions of the participants in the Boston Tea Party.

Designing Quality Homework Tasks

Designing quality homework tasks requires attention to four aspects, each of which affects students' motivation to approach the task and their perseverance in completing it:

• *Academic purpose*—Tasks should have a clear academic purpose.

• *Competence*—Tasks should have a positive effect on a student's sense of competence.

- *Ownership*—Tasks should be personally relevant and customized to promote ownership.
- *Aesthetics*—Tasks should be aesthetically pleasing.

Academic Component

Students often do not complete homework simply because the task is not meaningful. The most egregious homework practice is to assign busywork or tasks of dubious academic value that do not reinforce existing knowledge or demonstrate a mastery of knowledge (Past, 2006). Writing out definitions of vocabulary words, taking notes while reading a novel, or coloring in a map may sound like good homework, but one might question whether those tasks actually help students learn (Bennett & Kalish, 2006). Tasks requiring rote memory must be thought through carefully, given the access to rote knowledge that is available today. Some rote tasks are valid, such as memorizing spelling and math facts, but others may be questionable, such as memorizing state capitals.

Sometimes busywork is born from the attitudes discussed in Chapter 1—that homework must be assigned regardless of the value of the task. Sometimes homework tasks are well-intentioned attempts to have students do something fun or interesting, but the academic focus is not apparent. (What, exactly, is the learning purpose of a word search or a diorama? What evidence of learning do those tasks show?) As teachers consider the academic purpose of a particular homework task, they should focus less on the quantity of work they are expecting and more on the quality, keeping the focus on mastery of essential concepts and skills (Jackson, 2009).

The ultimate goal of the assignment—prelearning, checking for understanding, practice, or processing—should be clearly communicated to the student (Marzano et al., 2001). Students should easily understand the value of the task or be told explicitly how it helps learning. It may be helpful for teachers to create sample statements to use with students when they assign specific tasks.

These may be explained orally or be written on the homework sheet itself. Some sample statements are shown in Figure 4.2.

Students should have no trouble connecting homework to classroom learning. Homework tasks that have clear academic outcomes are well organized and easy to understand, preferably with written (not oral) directions.

Competence Component

One of the goals of homework is to ensure that students will feel positive about learning and develop an identity as successful

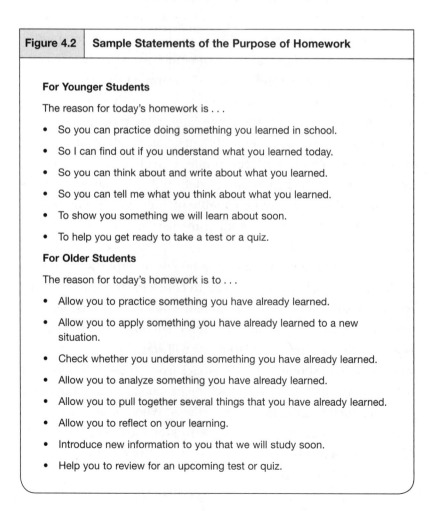

Figure 4.2	Sample Statements of the Purpose of Homework

For Younger Students

The reason for today's homework is . . .

- So you can practice doing something you learned in school.
- So I can find out if you understand what you learned today.
- So you can think about and write about what you learned.
- So you can tell me what you think about what you learned.
- To show you something we will learn about soon.
- To help you get ready to take a test or a quiz.

For Older Students

The reason for today's homework is to . . .

- Allow you to practice something you have already learned.
- Allow you to apply something you have already learned to a new situation.
- Check whether you understand something you have already learned.
- Allow you to analyze something you have already learned.
- Allow you to pull together several things that you have already learned.
- Allow you to reflect on your learning.
- Introduce new information to you that we will study soon.
- Help you to review for an upcoming test or quiz.

learners. Homework tasks should be designed not only to support classroom learning but also to instill a sense of competence in the mind of the learner (Sagor, 2002, 2008). In fact, when students feel unsuccessful in approaching homework tasks, they often avoid the tasks completely as a way to protect their self-esteem (Past, 2006). A major problem with homework is the demotivating effect of tasks that students are unable to complete on their own (Darling-Hammond & Ifill-Lynch, 2006). Homework that cannot be done without help is not good homework.

Failure-oriented students are particularly sensitive about how they feel about approaching a task. If certain tasks reinforce their view of themselves as "smarter," they will more likely attempt those tasks (Sagor, 2002, 2008). Being successful at completing homework feeds students' sense of competence. They will avoid tasks that make them feel "dumber" to protect their self-esteem (Glasser, 1992). This avoidance tendency means that for struggling students, hard tasks should come later, after they have accomplished easier tasks and feel confident in approaching homework. Poor grades on homework contribute to "feeling judged" and to a sense of failure, which increases anxiety and often causes students to avoid tasks they may be capable of successfully completing (Past, 2006). (The effects of grading are discussed at greater length later in the chapter.)

Just as checking for understanding is an important purpose for homework, teachers also need to check for frustration. Some will say frustration is good for students—that they must learn to work through it, that it builds character. But how much frustration is too much? At some point, students will shut down and refuse to work. Teachers should solicit feedback from students, finding out how students feel about approaching certain tasks and how they feel after they've attempted those tasks. When homework is not completed, teachers should talk with students to find out why. (Tools and methods to assist teachers in gathering this feedback are discussed in Chapter 5.)

Ownership Component

Students are often unmotivated to do homework because it is not perceived as important. It's just a task to do with no personal relevance or individuality. What's wrong with this picture? In many classrooms, students feel little or no ownership of their learning in general—we teach, we assign tasks, we test, and students are the passive receptacles (Eisner, 2003–2004; Intrator, 2004; Patterson, 2003). They have no stake in the outcome—it doesn't mean anything to them—because it's not about them. As long as learning and homework are being "done to" them, the goals are ours, not theirs (Kohn, 2006; Vatterott, 2007). As a teacher once said, "I've never heard of a child not doing *his* work; it's *our* work he's not doing."

Given the knowledge we now have about developmental needs, brain-based research, motivation, learning styles, and failure orientation, it seems obvious that the locus of control for homework must reside in the student. "Research suggests that homework must be increasingly inspired by students' own interests and motivations" (Corno, 1996, p. 29). If we claim that we want students to take responsibility for homework, we must give them more control over what they learn, how they learn it, and how they show that they've learned it (Guskey & Anderman, 2008). Students need and desire power over their own learning and are motivated by the prospect of choice and the opportunity for personal expression (Vatterott, 2007). Students must have opportunities to self-evaluate, to reflect on their own learning, and to set their own goals (Costa & Kallick, 2004; Guskey & Anderman, 2008). (Promoting student self-assessment is discussed later in this chapter.)

Often, when students will not do homework, we fail to examine the learning task we have given them to do. Instead of asking, "How do we get them to do their homework?" we should be asking, "What's the task?" (Darling-Hammond & Ifill-Lynch, 2006; Kohn, 1999, 2006). Quality tasks allow students the freedom to work from their strengths and create presentations or products that express their unique personal signature (Eisner, 2002). Students are most likely to be emotionally engaged by tasks that allow them to give their opinion, solve a problem that is important to them, compete with others, imagine possibilities, or be creative (Intrator, 2004; Vatterott, 2007). Students connect personally with the content when they identify with people or feelings, connect the content to something in their everyday life, use the content to understand the world around them, or wrestle with moral or ethical dilemmas (Vatterott, 2007).

Quality homework tasks promote ownership when they

- Allow for choices.
- Offer students an opportunity to personalize their work.
- Allow students to share information about themselves or their lives.
- Tap emotions, feelings, or opinions about a subject.
- Allow students to create products or presentations. (Vatterott, 2007)

The following are some examples of homework tasks that encourage student ownership:

- Students design their own method for learning multiplication tables that they then share with others—making cards; writing; reading; drawing pictures; or creating a song, rap, or poem.
- Students write a story or newspaper article showing that they know the meaning of the 15 vocabulary words for the week.
- Students create a *Jeopardy!* game that covers the main ideas at the end of a unit.
- Students write directions that can be used by other students for how to use a double balance beam.
- Students create a board game that illustrates the significant events of the Middle Ages. (Vatterott, 2007)

Aesthetic Component

We know that students differ in their preferred learning environment—for example, preferring either formal or informal settings, high or low light levels, or quiet or less quiet backgrounds (Dunn, 2003). Although those things may not matter to some students, for others those aspects of the task strongly affect motivation and the willingness to attempt the task. Just as some individuals are more sensitive to the aesthetics of their environment, some are also more sensitive to the aesthetics of the homework tasks they are assigned (Minotti, 2005). Closely related to the student's need for ownership, the aesthetic component refers to the *presentation* of the task—how enjoyable or engaging the task appears, as well as the visual appearance.

Gourmet cooks often insist that presentation is everything. Presentation is important for homework too. The *presentation* of homework is about how *appealing* the task is judged to be—the way it looks on paper; whether it appears easy or hard, fun or tedious, interesting or boring. Presentation is probably most important to younger students and academically challenged students. For example, students with learning disabilities often react more positively to assignments that are visually uncluttered. Such students are easily overwhelmed by spaces that are too small to write answers in or worksheets that have too much information on a page. Use of color, pictures, graphics, and other visual interests affects the way students feel about approaching a task. Remember the first time you had to read a book without pictures? Textbook publishers have long respected the importance of presentation in the design and marketing of textbooks.

Differentiating Homework Tasks

Because homework is completed independently, motivation becomes a huge issue. As with classroom instruction, homework must be differentiated based on the learner's unique profile of readiness, interests, learning style, organizational skills, and emotional factors such as motivation and persistence (Margolis, 2005; Minotti, 2005; Tomlinson, 1999).

While quality in homework tasks is important to motivation, differentiating homework tasks is critical to ensuring that students can be academically successful. Educators have long understood that when students feel competent as learners, they are more motivated to approach learning tasks—success breeds success, and failure is demotivating (Corno, 1996; Sagor, 2002).

It is obvious that learners differ in readiness and may vary in their pace and development of intellectual skills. As teachers come to acknowledge and embrace those differences in speed and style, they must communicate their respect for those differences to students. Learning is not about whether one student's *A* equals another student's *A,* but about each student's mastery of concepts and standards. Differentiating homework tasks allows the teacher to meet the individual needs of the students. Students who have been successful learners need to continue with increasingly challenging material and to maintain the confidence to learn new concepts and skills. Faster learners may need to be assigned more independent work or extended research. Students with severe disabilities must be given tasks at which they can be successful so that they will persevere (Frieman, 2001). Equally at risk, English language learners (ELLs) must be allowed to experience success in their native language until they are able to learn in English (Gebhard, 2002–2003). In addition, students with learning difficulties must be convinced that they can be capable learners and that their deficits can be remediated with hard work (Vatterott, 2007). This academic remediation is absolutely essential to those students' continued engagement in school. If students do not believe they are successful learners in elementary and middle school, they are at greater risk of dropping out of high school (Thornburgh, 2006; Wheelock & Dorman, 1988).

How can homework be differentiated? To meet the needs of a variety of learners, most teachers differentiate homework in one of three ways: by difficulty or amount of work, by the amount of structure or scaffolding provided, or by learning style or interest.

Differentiating by Difficulty or Amount of Work

Homework tasks that are too difficult for students to complete are a major demotivator for many students, especially academically challenged students (Tomlinson, 2003; Vatterott, 2003). To keep students motivated and willing to approach homework, tasks must be differentiated by level of difficulty. Students differ in their ability to understand concepts or in their skill level with particular tasks. Diagnosing and determining that readiness helps teachers answer this question: What level of work can the student successfully complete? This determination may be done through pre-tests, by observation of the students' understanding during class, or from their performance on previous homework.

Students with limited readiness may need homework involving simpler reading material or tasks that are more concrete. Instead of reading the textbooks, some students may use adapted reading packets that come with the text, which outline the main ideas of each chapter. More advanced students may benefit from more challenging tasks or the opportunity to explore topics in greater depth (Tomlinson, 1999).

For example, in Laura Eberle's high school physical science class, a homework assignment involved eight questions to demonstrate understanding of kinetic and potential energy. All students were expected to complete those questions. A challenge question was also given. All students were encouraged to attempt the challenge question, but only the students taking geometry were *required* to complete the challenge question. Laura explains: "I expect all kids to at least attempt the challenge problems, to show what formula to use. But as far as manipulating the math, I don't expect a pre-algebra kid to be able to do that math. It's multiple steps with harder vocabulary."

Closely related to difficulty, and equally important, is the *amount* of work students are assigned. The same task that takes the average student 15 minutes to complete could take another student more than an hour, causing some students to spend excessive time on homework. On the other hand, students who quickly and easily master concepts may become frustrated if asked to complete the same number of practice problems as students who have not yet mastered a concept. A simple means of differentiation is to ask all students to complete what work they can in a specific amount of time: "Do what you can in 20 minutes; draw a line, and work longer if you like." This approach provides valuable feedback to the teacher about working speed and level of understanding. Laura Eberle tells her high school science students, "If it's taking you more than 15 minutes to get it done, that's a red flag. You didn't pay attention or you don't have the notes—there's something wrong. No homework assignment should take longer than 10 to 15 minutes."

Molly Heckenberg's rule for her 5th graders' homework is "50 minutes is 50 minutes." Students are not expected to work more than 50 minutes each night. If students have homework in math, science, and reading and they spend 50 minutes on science and math, parents simply write a note saying, "We spent our 50 minutes on science and math and had no time for reading tonight."

Decisions about how many problems to assign or how many pages to read must consider the student's working speed as well as motivation and persistence. Because academically challenged learners are easily discouraged, care must be taken to limit the amount of work to what the student can complete in a reasonable amount of time.

Many teachers have discovered that the rate of homework completion skyrockets when they simply give less work. Most students are eager to be successful when the difficulty and amount of work are reasonable.

Which brings us to a dilemma. How do we find more time for slower learners?

Often, teachers expect slower learners to simply spend more time on homework than other students. The quandary is that slower learners usually are less persistent, tire more quickly, and often have less resilience with academic tasks. Like everyone, slow learners need downtime. With only so much time in a day, it seems unfair for slower learners not to "have a life." Special education professor Deb Childs recommends we "whittle down the curriculum to the concepts we believe are so essential they will remember them a year later" (personal communication, September 10, 2007). When differentiating for slower learners, the first questions teachers should ask are these: Are we doing the most efficient thing? Have we accurately diagnosed the student's readiness and learning strengths? Have we as teachers failed to connect cognitively with the student's learning style? Does the student need a more structured task? These questions lead us to two other methods of differentiating homework: providing structure or scaffolding, and differentiating by learning style or interest.

Differentiating by Amount of Structure or Scaffolding

Adding structure to homework tasks may help some students, especially struggling students and ELL students. Providing structure or scaffolding can help students feel the job is within their capabilities and can be completed without frustration. One of the simplest ways to help students is to require less writing, giving them assignments with fewer blanks to fill in or with answers that can be circled instead of written out. Many struggling students have poor fine-motor skills, which makes writing tedious.

Some students may be expected to create a graphic organizer of their reading, and others may be provided with the skeleton of an organizer and be required to fill in only a few key ideas. Some students may be given a word bank for answering questions or a copy of class notes to help them study. Class notes may be provided by the teacher or by another student. Math homework may be given with a choice of correct answers, or math manipulatives may be loaned out for homework. Teachers may allow some students to use a peer helper whom they can call if they have problems with homework. Hint sheets or lists of supplemental Web sites can also be given.

For some students, cursive writing makes assignments more difficult. Developmentally delayed elementary students and ELL students often struggle with cursive writing. Directions for homework may be printed instead of given in cursive writing. Instead of integrating practice in cursive writing with content assignments (asking students to translate their thoughts into cursive), teachers may choose to let students print or type content assignments and then practice their cursive writing separately.

ELL students may benefit from assignments with pictures and may find it easier to complete assignments in their native language first. Those assignments can be translated later by the student, a bilingual peer, or a bilingual teacher or aide. This approach allows the student to concentrate on one skill at a time. Similarly, when learning a multistep math process, students with limited readiness may need to master steps one at a time instead of mastering the entire process.

Differentiating by Learning Style or Interest

As discussed earlier, students enjoy choices and the ability to express their individuality. Adapting homework assignments to students' learning styles or interests is a quick path to fostering a sense of ownership of the homework task.

One of the easiest ways to capitalize on learning styles is to allow students to choose which method they will use to demonstrate what they have learned. Students may write, type, tape-record, or use pictures. Students may also decide which is the best way for them to practice rote memory tasks. For instance, instead of all students writing spelling words three times, students could be asked to design their own method for memorizing the words. Some may do it verbally, some by typing or writing, others by tracing the letters with their finger. Tactile learners may benefit from cards with raised images made from sandpaper-like material to learn such concepts as letters, geometric shapes, or geographic features. Figure 4.3 shows examples of how homework can be differentiated.

Figure 4.3	What Differentiated Homework Looks Like			
Purpose of Homework	**Example of Skill or Content**	**Differentiation for Difficulty/ Amount of Work**	**Differentiation for Scaffolding/Structure**	**Differentiation for Learning Style/Interest**
Rote memory practice	Multiplication tables	Some students may work on only one set at a time until they achieve some mastery. Other students may work on several sets at one time.	Some students may have a completed grid that they trace. Some students may write from memory.	Students may chose to write, recite, create their own table, or set tables to music to help them learn.
Practice of a skill	Division of whole numbers	Some students' problems may use two-digit numbers, some three-digit numbers, some four-digit numbers. Some students may be assigned fewer problems.	Some students may receive problems that are partially filled in—they provide the missing numbers. Some students may have explanations of steps written in the margin of their assignment.	Students may write and solve their own word problems, or they may complete practice problems from one of several math Web sites.
Prelearning	Main ideas of the chapter	Some students may have abbreviated reading assignments focusing only on certain sections of the chapter. Some may have focused questions to guide them to main ideas.	An advance organizer may be given to some students. Some may have a word bank to choose main ideas from.	Students may draw a graphic summary of the main ideas and list the three most interesting things about the chapter.
Check for understanding	Causes and effects of the Boston Tea Party	Some students will read the textbook. Other students may read a simpler version written as a play.	Some students may be asked to list the causes and effects of the Boston Tea Party. Other students may receive a list with some causes or some effects provided and have to fill in the blanks.	Students may be asked to defend or criticize the actions of the participants of the Boston Tea Party with an editorial, a poster, or a concept map.

Moving from Grading to Checking: Focusing on Feedback

All homework can be used to check for understanding if we can convince students not to be threatened by grades. The purpose of homework should be to provide feedback to the teacher and the student about how learning is progressing. The purpose is all about what informs learning and what informs the teacher. As we move into the feedback mode, we use completed assignments to revise future assignments (Popham, 2008). Feedback that revises instruction is often missing in the old paradigm. This omission is why the new paradigm changes the role of grading.

Grades are not necessary for learning to take place. In fact, research indicates that grades tend to interfere with learning (Guskey, 2003). Grades on homework often get in the way of learning, demotivate students, and create power struggles between students and teachers and between students and parents. Grading is viewed as evaluative by students—the teacher is perceived as a judge (Guskey, 2003). Checking (providing feedback) is diagnostic—the teacher is working as an advocate for the student. Should all homework be graded? No. Should all homework receive feedback? Yes.

Feedback as Assessment *for* Learning

Homework's role should be as formative assessment—assessment *for* learning that takes place *during* learning. Homework's role is not assessment *of* learning; therefore, it should not be graded. As a teacher who was also a coach once said about homework, "We don't keep score during practice." The goal of feedback on homework is to improve learning, to improve performance on summative assessments, to promote student ownership of learning, and to encourage self-assessment. "When homework is used as a formative assessment, students have multiple opportunities to practice, get feedback from the teacher, and improve" (Christopher, 2007–2008, p. 74). "Good formative assessment gives students information they need to understand where they are in their learning (the cognitive factor) and develops students' feelings of control over their learning (the motivational factor)" (Brookhart, 2007–2008, p. 54).

Focusing on feedback requires downsizing. Education consultant and author Grant Wiggins once said, "Teachers spend too much time teaching." Concerned about covering a glutted curriculum, teachers often become too focused on coverage to assess what students are actually mastering. Downsizing requires teachers to have clear goals, to prioritize concepts and skills for mastery, and to pare down content to a manageable amount. Focusing on feedback requires teacher to slow down—to teach less, assess more, and make time for reteaching some students or providing other students with additional assistance.

For many teachers, providing feedback without grades is a new way of communicating progress. They've never done school without grades, and for many of them, grades are the only way they know to give feedback. Letters and numbers are easy and fast, and they make up a language everyone *thinks* they understand. But there's a whole network of communication that many teachers are unaccustomed to using. Good feedback on homework requires back-and-forth dialogue between the teacher and the student, each asking questions of the other (orally or in writing). "Some of the best feedback results from conversations *with* the student" (Brookhart, 2007–2008, p. 55).

Efficient Ways of Providing Feedback

Busy teachers need strategies to help them efficiently create that dialogue. They need quick and efficient methods of checking for understanding—even if those methods are less than perfect. High school science teacher Laura Eberle explains her process: "I take 30 to 40 seconds to glance down, I see if it's complete, and I glance at their answers a bit. It doesn't take that long to get a general idea of where their hang-ups are. I do use [homework] as feedback for myself and what are they getting and what they are not."

Teachers who provide feedback efficiently often use their subjective judgment. Fifth grade teacher Molly Heckenberg does a quick visual check of homework each morning while her students are working on another task. She scans each assignment and put the papers into two piles—students who appear to have understood the concept and students who didn't. Without marking papers, she then knows how to regroup students, reteach, or assign students to buddy pairs to go over concepts again. Similarly, 3rd grade teacher Ken Pribish explains his procedure:

> Other teachers say, "How do you do that? It takes so much time." It takes less than five minutes a day to correct homework because I'm not "*correcting* homework." I'm looking at it to see if they did a good job, if they understood. Then I know I've got to meet with these three kids because they did not get last night's concept.

Increasingly, teachers are checking homework only for completion, not taking off points for incorrect answers. Many teachers use some sort of stamp to indicate complete or incomplete, on time or late. Laura Eberle gives a full stamp for completed work and a half stamp for incomplete work. Sixth grade communication arts teacher Shannon Burger gives formative feedback on student notebooks with a symbol stamp; each time she checks the notebooks she uses a different symbol, such as a bear or a dog. A right-side-up symbol signifies a good job, a sideways symbol signifies an OK job, and an upside-down symbol signifies the work is not adequate.

On specific projects such as essays, teachers may keep a list of common positive and negative statements they wrote on student projects one semester: "good use of descriptive words," "punctuation used correctly," "did not use correct grammar," or "ideas do not flow well." From those, the teacher can create a list of comments, similar to a rubric, that can then quickly be checked off, with space for other comments as well.

Teachers are not the only ones who can provide feedback. Feedback can also be given from student to student. Often, teachers will simply ask students to meet in groups to compare their homework answers, ask each other questions, and then report back to the teacher. The group discussions are often quite valuable; the back-and-forth conversation helps students clarify the goals of the assignment.

Moving from grading to feedback encourages student ownership of learning. Allowing students to take control of their learning makes learning personal (Guskey & Anderman, 2008). "Students decide whether the learning is worth the risk and effort required to acquire it. They decide if they believe they are smart enough to learn it" (Stiggins, 2005, p. 18). Once the threat of grades is taken away from the homework experience, "homework becomes a safe place to try out new skills without penalty, just as athletes and musicians try out their skills on the practice field or in rehearsals" (Christopher, 2007–2008, p. 74).

When teachers stop grading homework, many of them see an attitudinal shift—students come to trust that teachers are working together with them to meet their learning needs, and they feel a sense of empowerment over their own learning (Popham, 2008). The move away from grading is a move from what Kohn (1998) calls the *demand* model to the *support* model. Instead of *demanding* that students do their homework under threat of bad grades or punishment, we actively *support* them in taking responsibility for their own learning—we *assist* them in learning. Moving from grading to checking requires a total attitudinal change by both teachers and students about what homework is for. It's not "gotcha," not grading, but feedback for students about *their understanding.* This shift in the locus of control of homework is initially scary for both students and teachers.

Students must overcome the hurdle of old-paradigm attitudes (Guskey & Anderman, 2008). Most students are so accustomed to experiencing assessment as reward and punishment, they at first tend to view even *corrective* feedback as judgmental. They "hear judgment where you intend description" (Brookhart, 2007–2008, p. 56). Unsuccessful students often bear scar tissue from negative grading experiences of the past. They view feedback as black and white, right or wrong. "Even well-intentioned feedback can be very destructive if the student reads the script in an unintended way" (Brookhart, 2007–2008, p. 54).

Teachers need to be especially sensitive to this dynamic; they need to choose feedback language carefully and balance positive and negative feedback. "Unsuccessful learners have sometimes been so frustrated by their school experience that they might see every attempt to help them as just another declaration that they are 'stupid'" (Brookhart, 2007–2008, p. 56). Students who have a history of failure on assessment fall into the homework trap discussed earlier and tend to shut down and refuse to work. But the trap is a problem for other students as well. Those students who have been following the rules face a bigger problem—they have internalized the external nature of assessment as something "done to" them (Kohn, 2006). Their perception of the grading process is this: "Did I guess correctly what you wanted?" In reading corrective feedback, students may think, "She didn't like it; it's not right" because the teacher did not make the feedback specific enough. Due to past experience, these students may have little sense of ownership of their learning, believing that it's all about giving the teacher what the teacher wants, what gets the grade (Pope, 2001).

Helping Students Self-Assess

Many students don't know how to self-assess because, as noted earlier, assessment has always been "done to" them. If they've been trained in a system of rote learning to just spit content back, then reflecting and evaluating their own learning is a foreign concept to them (Guskey & Anderman, 2008). They need ungraded, nonthreatening practice to get used to the concept. They need

scaffolded strategies to self-assess, to check for their own understanding, and to follow their own progress.

High-achieving students use a variety of ways to check
themselves for understanding. They may restate sections of the
material or ask themselves questions about the material. When
struggling students were able to observe and adopt similar self-
checking strategies, they showed significant improvement in
comprehension (Fisher & Frey, 2007). Once students learn how
to take control of their own assessment, they feel more positive
about their learning. "Students commented that self-assessment
helped them feel prepared, improved the quality of their work,
and gave them a better understanding of what they had achieved"
(Andrade, 2007–2008, p. 60).

Teachers can begin by asking students to rate how well they
understood a homework assignment. This rating allows students
to reflect on the homework task and to provide information to
the teacher. Students can use one of three symbols or stickers
at the top of the homework assignment to indicate their level of
understanding:

Got it/understood	!/happy face/green sticker
Sort of got it/not sure	?/neutral face/yellow sticker
Didn't get it/totally lost	#&/frowning face/red sticker

Teacher Angela Saracino gets feedback from homework by asking
her 1st graders to circle the part of the spelling word that is the
trickiest. Then she uses that feedback to explain spelling rules to
her students.

Another way to help students self-assess is to assign test
corrections as homework after a test. For each question students got wrong, they must state why they missed the question.
They must then find the correct answer in their notes or book.
Students can regain some lost points on their test grade when
they turn in test corrections. A student example is shown in
Figure 4.4.

Figure 4.4	Test Correction Activity	
Item Number	**Reason Missed**	**Corrected and Found**
#6	Misunderstood the book	D. page 4 "survived <u>primarily</u> by hunting large game" (key word "primarily")
#11	Careless mistake	E. page 7
#15	Knowledge (didn't know when they abandoned their homes)	E. pages 9–10
#22	Misunderstood question (thought "attitude" was "altitude")	E. page 19

Another way to help students self-assess is to have them respond to reflective questions such as these suggested by Tomlinson and McTighe (2006, p. 25):

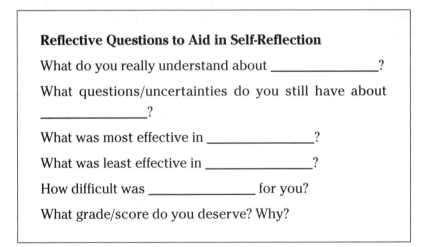

Reflective Questions to Aid in Self-Reflection

What do you really understand about _____?

What questions/uncertainties do you still have about _____?

What was most effective in _____?

What was least effective in _____?

How difficult was _____ for you?

What grade/score do you deserve? Why?

Decriminalizing the Grading of Homework

If moving from grading to checking is so positive and empowering for students, why would we bother to grade homework at all? Actually many teachers around the world do not grade homework. In a comparison of 50 countries, U.S. teachers lead the world in the grading of homework. Almost 70 percent of U.S. teachers use homework to calculate student grades, compared with 28 percent in Canada and 14 percent in Japan (Baker & LeTendre, 2005). As discussed earlier, grading plays a huge role in the old homework paradigm; homework grades are used to reward the virtue of turning work in on time and to punish the vice of perceived laziness—so much so that teachers will say, "If I don't grade it, they won't do it." Yet even with grades, some students fail to complete homework. And in schools in which homework is not graded, students are still expected to complete it, and teachers still struggle to find ways to get the work done. Grading is so much a part of the old paradigm that teachers may become very upset at the idea of *not grading* homework.

* * *

The Concept of Grading Homework Dies Hard

In one district, high school teachers who counted homework heavily in the grades they gave protested when the middle school decided not *to count homework in grades. The high school teachers believed that if the middle school didn't count homework as part of the grade or if they allowed students to redo homework, they would be setting the students up for failure in the high school because homework* did *count in the high school grades. What was particularly interesting was how passionately teachers felt about the necessity of grading homework.*

"At the last meeting, one high school teacher about jumped out of her skin. The idea that every homework assignment wouldn't count as part of the final grade was inconceivable," according to another teacher. Members of the district committee worked hard to convince other teachers that grades must be based on whether or not the students learned *what they were supposed to. The committee finally agreed that behaviors should not be part of grades and that pre-tests, first attempts, and practice should not be averaged into the grade.*

* * *

The goal is to have grades reflect learning, not behavior or personal responsibility. As one teacher said, "What if grades reflected what students really learned, not which work they chose or were able to complete?" Decriminalizing homework is an attempt to make that happen. The general philosophy is this: First, do no harm—don't kill motivation or course grades by being too punitive. Teachers in schools and in individual classrooms around the world are taking steps to deemphasize the grading of homework, as evidenced in the following trends:

• Some schools are not allowing homework to be counted in the grade.

• Some schools are limiting the percentage that homework may count in the final grade, often to 10 percent.

• Some schools are allowing teachers to give *incomplete* grades when all homework has not been completed.

• Some schools have adopted Zeros Aren't Possible (ZAP) policies—requiring that all work must be completed. (See Chapter 5 to learn more.)

• Individual teachers are revising their own grading schemes to limit the percentage that homework counts (often 10 to 20 percent).

• Some teachers are giving credit for completion only, not correctness or accuracy of the work.

• Some teachers are using the percentage of homework assignments completed for the quarter as the total grade for homework for that quarter.

• Some teachers are using homework as extra credit, but not part of the regular grade.

An example of the last trend is Teresa Schultz's 8th grade math class, where homework can add 5 percentage points to the student's grade if the student is missing no more than two assignments. The percentage added decreases as students are missing more assignments. If they are missing six assignments, they get to add only 1 percentage point. In one teacher's opinion, "If you give homework a lot of value, you encourage cheating."

● ● ●

Questions—And More Questions

"If homework counts as only 10 percent of the grade, then what would we grade?" This question arose from teachers in a staff development session about homework, which led the presenter to ask this question: "What are teachers grading?" It appeared that some teachers at this school graded only tests and homework. Why weren't they grading tasks that students did in class? Perhaps because they were primarily lecturing and having discussions and not providing many learning activities during class time that could be evaluated.

This led to a broader discussion. "What are you doing with grades? What do grades mean to you?" The discussion with this group of teachers revealed a larger problem. They viewed grades as a commodity—they needed a certain number of grades in the gradebook to feel secure. They needed a certain number of grades to please parents. They just needed to make sure they had enough things to grade. What they had failed to consider was whether the grades represented learning and how many grades students needed in order to know how they were doing. The teachers had failed to focus on which tasks accurately reflected student learning.

● ● ●

Decriminalizing Late Policies

If the purpose of homework is to enhance learning and provide feedback about learning, then the goal is for the homework to be completed—better late than never. But for some teachers, homework is more about their control and convenience than about learning. One teacher explained, "I will not accept late work past two days. Any later and the students end up creating their own time schedule, do what they want when they want, and it's not worth (time-wise) going back and grading something you've moved past." For those teachers who feel compelled to punish the vice of lateness, there is a kinder, gentler way than the old policy that says "50 percent off if it's one day late." Policies like that are an insult to the time and energy the student put forth to complete the assignment. Many a student has simply said, "No way—I am not doing that much work for half credit," and the assignment is never done.

Work completed deserves some credit. To encourage students to do the work, it's better to provide a more generous time limit with fewer points lost than to punish the student for not following the rules. Remember that the goal is learning, not control or compliance.

For teachers who feel they must penalize lateness, it is best to separate grades for learning from grades for work habits (Guskey & Anderman, 2008). Here is one way to do that. Suppose there are 100 points possible for each homework assignment. Completion of each assignment could be worth 80 points, and work habits could be worth 20 points if the assignment is turned in on time. Rather than docking points for each day the assignment is late (a bookkeeping nightmare for the teacher), there are only three possibilities for the work habits grade—20 points for turning the assignment in on time, 10 points if turned in within a week, 0 points if turned in after a week. With this method, the student gets full credit for doing the work but is penalized only slightly for the work being late.

Figure 4.5 shows an example of three students' grades for homework. Amy turned in all homework on time, Jack turned in all assignments within a week, and Alex's assignments were all more than a week late.

Ninth grade science teacher Laura Eberle has a system that works well. She gives a small amount of homework, and she grades for completion only. Her policy, shown here, connects the purpose of the homework to class tests:

Figure 4.5	The 80/20 Homework Grade		
Student & Assignment	Completion (80 points max.)	Work Habits (20 points max.)	Total/Cumulative Total (100/500 points max.)
Amy			
Assignment #1	80	20	100
Assignment #2	80	20	100
Assignment #3	80	20	100
Assignment #4	80	20	100
Assignment #5	80	20	100
Cumulative total			**500**
Jack			
Assignment #1	80	10	90
Assignment #2	80	10	90
Assignment #3	80	10	90
Assignment #4	80	10	90
Assignment #5	80	10	90
Cumulative total			**450**
Alex			
Assignment #1	80	0	80
Assignment #2	80	0	80
Assignment #3	80	0	80
Assignment #4	80	0	80
Assignment #5	80	0	80
Cumulative total			**400**

Full stamp = 10 points   Completed and turned in on time, full credit.

Half stamp = 5 points   Turned in on time, but incomplete. Complete it before the day of the test and earn 7 points.

No stamp = 0 points   Not turned in on time. Complete it before the day of the test and earn 5 points.

As more and more schools move to standards-based report cards, homework grades may become obsolete. If the goal is mastery of the standard, would it matter if or when homework was completed? Mastery of standards would be based on in-class assessments, with homework used to prepare students to pass the assessment. Homework would be necessary only to master individual standards; if students tested out of some standards, no homework would be necessary for that content.

Summing Up

Most teachers were never trained in effective homework practices. As a result, traditional practices, such as assigning the same homework to all students and giving zeros for incomplete homework, are still common. Many of those traditional practices, however, have not supported learning for all students. The new homework paradigm introduced in this chapter focuses on designing quality homework tasks, differentiating those tasks, deemphasizing grading, improving homework completion, and providing homework support programs.

Homework should not occur in isolation but should be closely connected to classroom learning. The purpose of homework is to *support* classroom learning through practice, prelearning, processing, or checking for understanding. When classroom learning and homework are carefully planned, the pieces of the puzzle fit together nicely; homework is used as *formative assessment*—to check for understanding before practice is assigned, to determine how much practice is needed to perfect a skill, and to judge the student's depth of understanding and ability to apply learning.

Viewing homework as formative feedback changes our perspective on the grading of homework. Grading becomes not only unnecessary for feedback, but possibly even detrimental to the student's continued motivation to learn. With this new perspective, incomplete homework is not punished with failing grades but is viewed as a symptom of a learning problem that requires investigation, diagnosis, and support. Strategies for improving homework completion and providing support programs are discussed in Chapter 5.

5

Homework Completion Strategies and Support Programs

Chapter 4 discussed the first four steps of the new homework paradigm: designing and differentiating quality homework tasks, moving from grading to checking, and decriminalizing grading. These strategies make homework tasks more pleasant and less punitive, and they increase student ownership of homework. These changes from traditional practice should make completion of homework less of an issue. In Chapter 5, we consider the last two steps in the new homework paradigm: strategies for homework completion and programs that support students in completing homework at school.

Attitudes About Homework Completion

Before we attempt to improve the rate of homework completion, we must confront one more traditional attitude. It is common for teachers to become obsessed with the fact that "all homework must be done." But does it truly need to be done? When it comes to learning, it's not about finishing the work; it's about demonstrating learning. Can students prove that they know what they need to know? How can we determine how well they are learning, and how can we help them do better? If we can assess learning without all those homework assignments and the students have learned what we wanted them to learn, we don't need the homework! This is a hard pill to swallow if we believe that students must do as they are told, and that not completing all homework is a sign of laziness or insubordination. But if we become so concerned that children have not been compliant, we lose sight of the role homework should play in learning. Focused on enforcing our own power as teachers, we become afraid to trust students, afraid they're going to "get away with something"—so we sometimes resort to punitive solutions that backfire.

Author and educational consultant Rick Wormeli raises an interesting point about homework. He asks, "Why do we expect 100 percent compliance in getting homework done on time? After all, we don't expect all students to get *A*s or all students to behave perfectly all the time" (personal communication, November 8, 2007).

Diagnosing Completion Problems

Often when students do not complete homework, the teacher's first concern is "How do I make them do it?" or to blame the students or their parents for not being compliant. Neither strategy gets to the root of the problem. The first step in improving homework completion is to diagnose why the homework is not getting done. There are usually five types of reasons:

- *Academic*—Task too hard or too lengthy for the student's working speed
- *Organizational*—Getting it home, getting it done, getting it back
- *Motivational*—Burnout, overload, too much failure, frustration with tasks
- *Situational*—Unable to work at home, too many other activities, no materials available at home for the assignment
- *Personal*—Depression, anxiety, family problems, or other personal issue

Academic and organizational issues may be easier to diagnose than motivational, situational, or personal issues; it often takes a bit of detective work to determine the problem.

For some students, incomplete homework is the result of procrastinating and then running out of time. Procrastination is simply a symptom of other problems. Upon closer investigation, we find that students procrastinate for different reasons, each needing a different solution. David, a 6th grader, puts off doing homework because the tasks he is assigned are boring and tedious. Jason, a 3rd grader, has both academic and motivational reasons for procrastinating. He avoids homework because the tasks are so difficult that he feels frustrated and incompetent. Amanda has organizational problems with long-range projects. As a 4th grader, she has had little experience or guidance in how to budget time and set intermittent deadlines for herself. At her age, time is an abstract concept, and three weeks seems like an infinite amount of time to finish a project. Nathan's problems are situational. As a popular 8th grader, he first makes time for sports and his social life, leaving little time for homework, his last priority.

For some students, procrastination is akin to a preferred learning style, almost part of their personality. Jennifer, a 9th grader who is often late for school and late with homework assignments, has what time management experts call "an ideal relationship with time." She estimates that ideally she can get ready for school in 15 minutes, can get to school in 10 minutes, and can complete that assignment in 30 minutes, when in reality it will take her much longer. Scott, a 12th grader, procrastinates because, like many adults, he focuses better under the pressure of tight deadlines, but sometimes he runs out of time.

Each student's situation is unique, and sometimes the student has more than one issue contributing to the problem. Take Laura, for instance. Laura was a bright, sociable 7th grader who just wouldn't keep up with her homework. Earlier in the school year, Laura seemed to be breezing right through the regular homework, so her academic team of teachers decided she should be doing more challenging homework instead. That's when the problems started. Laura seemed to take no initiative to do the work yet appeared to feel guilty when she did not have homework to turn in. She was testing poorly. Her parents claimed she locked herself in her room for four hours a night doing homework. (They seemed powerless to monitor whether she was actually working during that time.) They promised to get more involved but did not. They continued to make excuses for why Laura was not completing homework (situational).

Upon further investigation, the team discovered Laura was struggling with the challenge homework (academic), was feeling overwhelmed (motivational), and was free to talk with friends or spend time in chat rooms while locked in her room (situational). Due to her lack of organization, she often completed work that never made it back to the teacher (organizational).

The teachers decided to take the parents out of the equation and deal directly with Laura. They followed three simple steps. First, they went back to giving her regular homework assignments instead of challenge work, at least until they reestablished the pattern of her getting all the work back and saw her test grades improve. Second, upon talking with Laura, they discovered that she didn't like to put work in folders as suggested by her teachers, and work often got lost as a result. When asked what might work better, she said she preferred to fold the work and put it in her textbook. This simple change helped Laura become more organized because it gave her the control she needed to do what made sense to her. Finally, because Laura was not self-motivated to complete work, the teachers assigned her to a mandatory after-school homework support program until she developed a track record of turning in all work. After that they periodically placed Laura back in the homework support program as needed, before she was missing too many assignments.

Whether the challenge work was too hard for Laura or whether she had too much going on in her life and could not focus was irrelevant. The work was not getting done, and she was not doing well on tests. Laura's story illustrates the need for teachers to step back when necessary and respect students' emotional needs.

Both academic and motivational reasons can be influenced by the type of homework tasks students are assigned. As teachers, we often assume that our homework tasks are irreplaceable—that it has to be *that task* that the student must complete. In fact, are there alternatives to the original task, perhaps shorter or different tasks that will accomplish the same result? If the role of the task is to promote learning, why can't students do a different task? If the role of the task is to measure learning, why can't we take a smaller measure or a different measure?

Diagnostic Tools

In many cases, a simple conversation with the student may give us the insight we need to diagnose the cause of problems with home-work completion. The tools described here can also be helpful.

Parent or student feedback checklists can help us determine how much time students are spending on homework and the reasons why work is not being completed. Using the checklists daily for a short period should reveal what difficulties the student is having. Depending on the age and maturity of the student and the level of involvement of the parent, the checklist may be directed to either the student or the parent. (See Figure 5.1 for a Student Feedback Checklist; a Parent Feedback Checklist is shown in Figure 2.4 in Chapter 2.)

A *home study plan* (see Figure 5.2) helps students reflect on the conditions under which they work best. It helps students and parents determine the best time and place for homework to be completed.

Taylor's Homework Chain (Figure 5.3) was created for students with attention deficit disorder, but it can be helpful for any student with organizational problems. It helps students to self-diagnose where organization is breaking down in the process of getting homework completed and turned in (Taylor, 2007).

Figure 5.1	Student Feedback Checklist

Student Feedback Checklist
(Attach to homework)

Dear student:

I estimate you can complete this assignment in _____ minutes.

It is not necessary for you to work longer than _____ minutes on this assignment, even if you do not finish it. You will not be penalized.

How much time did you spend on this assignment?_____

If you did not finish the assignment, please check the reason or reasons why below:

_____ I could no longer focus on the task.

_____ I was too tired.

_____ I did not understand the assignment.

_____ I did not have the necessary materials to complete the assignment.

_____ I did not have enough time due to other outside activities.

_____ Other reason (please explain). _____

_____

_____

Student signature

Prioritizing Concepts, Tasks, and Subjects

If, after diagnosis and adjustment of homework for a student's specific needs, the student is still consistently not completing all work, it may be that the student is a slow worker. In that case, it may be necessary to prioritize concepts within a subject. Prioritizing can be done by identifying mastery and nonmastery concepts and, when the student begins to get behind, excusing some of the nonmastery concepts. Some teachers feel this is letting students

Figure 5.2	Home Study Plan

We all have ways we like to work. These questions will help you figure out the best way to do homework. Circle the answer that is most like you. (For prereaders, read questions and have students draw their answers.)

1. My favorite position to do homework is . . .

    At a desk.

    Sitting on the floor.

    Standing.

    Lying down.

2. It is easiest for me to pay attention to homework . . .

    In a quiet place.

    With noise or music in the background.

3. When I am working on homework . . .

    I need to have something to eat or drink.

    I don't need to have drinks or food.

4. When I have more than one thing to do . . .

    I like to do the easiest thing first.

    I like to do the hardest thing first.

5. After I start working, I like to . . .

    Work for a long time before I take a break.

    Work for a short time, take a break, then work more.

6. When is it easiest for me to do homework?

    I like to work as soon as I get home from school.

    I need to play or relax for a little while and then work.

    I need a long break after school before I am ready to work.

7. Where will I do homework?

    I can work in the same place every day and can keep my homework things there. That place is_____.

    I have to work in different places on different days, so I need to keep my homework things in a box that I can move. Some of the places I will work are _____ _____.

Figure 5.3	Taylor's Homework Chain

Which links are weak or broken?

[ ] 1. Realize an assignment is being given.

[ ] 2. Understand the assignment.

[ ] 3. Record the assignment accurately.

[ ] 4. Understand how to perform the assignment correctly.

[ ] 5. Check to bring correct books home.

[ ] 6. Arrive home with materials and the homework assignment.

[ ] 7. Begin the homework session.

[ ] 8. Complete all homework.

[ ] 9. Check that it is complete, accurate, and neat.

[ ] 10. Set completed homework in a special place.

[ ] 11. Take completed homework to school.

[ ] 12. Arrive at class with completed homework.

[ ] 13. Turn completed homework in on time.

Source: From *Motivating the Uncooperative Student: Redeeming Discouragement and Attitude Problems,* by Dr. John Taylor, 2007, Monmouth, OR: ADD Plus. Copyright © 2007 by ADD Plus. Adapted with permission.

off too easy, but if the students are slower learners, they simply may not have enough time. A useful analogy might be this: Suppose a student missed a month of school because he was sick. Wouldn't we just excuse some work and grade him only on what he had done? Or wouldn't we penalize him ever so slightly so he could still get a decent grade?

One teacher made this comment: "If you prioritize tasks, you'll probably realize the task at the bottom of the list isn't worth doing and should be dropped." For students with multiple learning deficits, prioritizing of homework in different subjects is essential to avoid overburdening the student. For each of those students, teachers must answer the following question: "What are the most critical subjects for future success?" For instance, if reading comprehension is a problem, it affects all content learning and must take priority. If basic math skills are hampering the student's ability to perform higher operations, those basic skills must be priorities. The dilemma comes in the prioritizing of individual academic subjects. Should math and reading be prioritized over science and social studies? Should homework in the four academic subjects be prioritized over homework in the elective subjects? The balancing of priorities is a difficult job that may require the collaboration of several teachers.

General Classroom Strategies for Homework Completion

All students benefit from a consistent routine such as having homework on the same days of the week, or always having math homework on Mondays and reading homework on Tuesdays. Younger students benefit from homework in the same format, such as five practice problems followed by five review problems.

Many students in elementary and middle school need help in organization. It is usually worth the time to teach students specific organizational strategies and to schedule a regular time for them to organize folders or clean out lockers. Middle school teachers who schedule weekly locker clean-outs find many homework assignments in the process! Some high school students still require this type of monitoring and organizational help.

A visual chart of completed homework is a concrete way for students to track their work. Having students keep an individual record or graph of how many assignments they have turned in on time is one approach. Laura Eberle keeps a copy of her 9th graders' homework grades on a wall poster. Students are identified with a PIN number they select. They can then check the chart at any time to see what assignments they may be missing. One 2nd grade teacher had students make a bar graph showing the number of students who turned in their homework each day. The simple visual of the bars seemed to improve the number of students who turned in work. The names of the students who did not turn in work were not revealed or placed on the graph, as that would have been punitive and embarrassing for those students.

If homework assignments are not written out on paper, wise teachers write the assignment on the board and check to make sure all students have copied the assignment. Soon the teacher knows exactly which students to check to see if they have copied the assignment. Some students may need to receive a written copy or to have a buddy write down the assignment for them.

Other strategies that may improve the rate of homework completion are the following:

- Limit homework to one assignment or one subject per night.
- Take time to discuss the homework assignment and possibly give students a few minutes to begin the assignment in class. This way, students can be sure they understand what they are supposed to do.
- Avoid giving homework assignments at the end of the hour, when students are packing up and focused on leaving.
- Set a maximum amount of time that the student should work on each assignment.
- Provide peer tutors or study groups for some students.
- Assign students homework buddies to work with or call for help.
- Give assignments further in advance of the due date, or give students more than one day to do assignments.
- Provide homework packets or lists of weekly or monthly assignments.
- Give all assignments for the next week on Friday, due the next Friday.
- Establish intermittent due dates for parts of long-term projects.
- Provide a course syllabus at the beginning of the semester with all homework listed.

- Allow some homework to lag two to three weeks behind the introduction of a concept to check for understanding (like a take-home test).
- Make sure all students have the necessary materials at home to complete specific assignments.

Here are some home-based strategies to improve completion of homework:

- Use the parent or student feedback checklists (Figures 2.4 and 5.1, respectively) for students who repeatedly have completion problems.
- Use the Home Study Plan (Figure 5.2) to help students create the best homework environment at home.
- Use Taylor's Homework Chain (Figure 5.3) to diagnose students with organizational problems.
- Use the Home Schedule Card for Parents (Figure 2.2) in Chapter 2 to determine if some students need more flexibility in homework deadlines.
- Give some students a copy of the textbook to keep at home.
- Allow parents or students to call the teacher at home when necessary.
- Have younger students make and decorate a "homework box" to keep materials in at home.
- Give parents specific guidelines on *how* to help with homework and *how much* to help (see example in Figure 2.1 in Chapter 2).

Using Incentives to Improve Homework Completion

Given the limitations of zeros and late policies, we have come to realize that it's pretty hard to punish students into doing homework. But the behaviorist mind-set dies hard, leading many teachers to ask, "Why not use *rewards* to get students to complete homework?" Rewards or incentive programs are often the last resort of a frustrated teacher. In fact, rewards may work in some situations and with some students, but the effects must be carefully thought out. Sometimes the unanticipated results of rewards make them undesirable.

Teachers often use incentive programs as a quick fix and therefore fail to explore why homework is not being completed. As discussed previously, because the reasons differ for individual children, so must the solutions. Incentive programs also tend to focus on "just doing it" without explaining to students why the assignments are important for either checking for understanding or improving learning.

When using incentives, teachers dangle the promise of tokens, treats, or free time to entice reluctant learners to complete their homework. For some students, the rewards work. But the biggest problem with rewards is the student who doesn't get the reward. The flip side of any reward is a punishment (Kohn, 1999). Consider the following example of a well-intentioned primary teacher.

Frustrated with the students who were not turning in homework, Ms. Hart instituted an incentive program. On random days, she would reward children who had all their homework turned in with a party of milk and cookies. The children who had not turned in their homework were required to work on their homework. When those students had completed their homework, they too received milk and cookies. "It's not a punishment if they are not doing *extra* work—they are just doing their work," Ms. Hart said. "But that's not how the kids will perceive it," another teacher said.

The other teacher was right. In this situation, three things made the lack of reward feel like a punishment. The first was providing food—a powerful reward and one of our basic human needs—while other students received no food until they were finished with their work. The second was calling it a "party"—who likes *not* being invited to a party? The third thing was that the students who had to work were in the same room as the partiers and had to work while watching the others party!

Most important, though, the strategy was ineffective in the long run. Why? Because almost every time, the same five students missed the party while working to catch up.

How could the teacher make this strategy less punitive? First, either nobody gets food or everybody gets food, even those students who have to catch up on their work (they can work and eat at the same time). Second, if possible, separate the groups in two different rooms. Maybe Ms. Hart could work with another teacher who also wanted students to have catch-up time. And finally, don't call it a "party"; call it "free time."

The best incentives relate to learning and minimize the difference between the reward and the punishment. The students who are given the reward of free time could be given only academic options—to read, to play a learning game, or to learn more about a topic of interest to them. That way, all students would be working on a learning task.

Battlefield Elementary School in Fort Oglethorpe, Georgia, experimented with a different solution. The school rearranged the schedule once a week to allow students who had completed all homework to have an extra physical education period. The students who had incomplete homework for the week stayed in the classroom and worked, while those who had turned in all assignments left the classroom for the gym.

Some teachers give students a reward for the number of assignments turned in on time. Rick Wormeli, a veteran teacher and staff developer, gives homework extension passes for every 5 out of 10 homework assignments turned in on time. Homework extension passes allow students to turn in future assignments late. Rick also recommends having students set goals either individually or in teams for on-time performance. Just as companies reward workers for meeting target goals, the teacher can reward students for meeting their own goals—for instance, turning in 80 percent of homework on time. This strategy, when used for individual students, gives the students some control over setting goals that they think will be doable for them. However, when used for teams of students it could be problematic, as one student's performance could affect the team's reward and cause problems among team members. The team's peer pressure would be effective only if all students in the group had the time, ability, and home environment necessary to complete homework.

For most students, the best incentives are short-term. In one elementary school, 5th graders had an end-of-the-year party. To qualify for the party, students had to meet specific requirements for behavior and had to have completed all work. Although the prospect of the party was enticing, only about half of the 5th graders qualified for the party one year, primarily because of incomplete homework. Why didn't this incentive work better? First of all, the promise of a reward several months in the future was too far away for many 5th graders. Second, because time was not available for students to make up work after school (the school had no activity buses), many students had no way to catch up when they got behind on homework. So the incentive was too long-term, and the requirement of completing 100 percent of the homework was too high a bar. Perhaps an adjustment in the requirements, such as a smaller party each quarter or requiring students to complete a minimum of 80 percent of their homework, could have resulted in more students qualifying for the party.

All incentive programs have the same potential drawback. What about the student who, for whatever reason, is unable to do homework at home? That student will never get the incentive, will never get the reward. Is that fair? That is why the more humane solution is the establishment of homework support programs, which provide a time and a place within the school for those students to successfully complete homework.

Establishing Homework Support Programs

Instead of trying to *teach* kids responsibility with late policies and failing grades, what if we forced them to *practice* responsibility? Teachers who use some of the completion strategies described earlier do this, as do teachers who stay after school or give up their lunch period to help students complete homework. School-sanctioned homework support programs extend that help in a broader, more organized fashion. Homework support programs make time for students to complete homework during or after school, with the following implication: "There's no *not* doing it. All homework must be completed." Homework support programs allow us to save students from themselves, to make it difficult for them to fail. Homework support programs allow us to "bird-dog" students to make sure they complete the work necessary to succeed. If they are inefficient or unmotivated learners, doesn't it make sense that they would need to do homework at school in a structured support program, where they could get expert one-on-one help? If students need extra help with homework, it is the obligation of the *school* to provide that help, not outside tutoring services.

But homework support programs are no magic bullet. Support programs focus on completion, but in isolation. They fail to take into account *why* students are not completing homework—the diagnosis is missing. Ideally, homework support programs should be used in conjunction with the previously discussed teacher strategies for differentiation, diagnosis, and completion. Also, homework support programs work only if students are given a reasonable amount of homework. If students are assigned several hours of nightly homework or if they are slow workers, a homework support program alone will not save them.

The most successful programs kick in when a student is missing only 2 or 3 assignments, not 9 or 10 assignments. Once students become backlogged with too many missing assignments, the job of catching up becomes laborious and the prospect of reaching the goal bleak.

The Philosophy Behind Successful Support Programs

A successful homework support program is not just about homework. It is a reflection of a school philosophy of high expectations for all, a respect for students' innate desire to succeed, and a comprehensive approach that actively monitors student performance and mandates additional help when needed (Perkins-Gough, 2006). It represents a no-excuses, whatever-it-takes attitude on the part of the faculty and administrators.

Boaz Middle School in Boaz, Alabama, is an excellent example of a school with a comprehensive approach. Although it is a Title I school, with 50 percent of students at poverty level, its standardized test scores are among the highest in the state, and for the past five years, no student has failed. Boaz Middle School has a daily reading period that allows intervention for struggling readers, writing and math integrated across the curriculum, a predominance of active learning over passive learning, and frequent cross-curricular projects. Each grade level has procedures in place that outline how unfinished homework will be completed, and there are several schoolwide programs available to teachers to ensure that all homework is completed (Pyron, 2008).

Homework support programs are more effective when the attitudes and intentions of teachers and administrators are about helping rather than punishing. Attitudes and intentions are revealed to students in formal policy statements about the support programs, in the way teachers communicate to students referred to the program, and in how students are treated when working in the program. The heart of a successful support program is just that—heart. It is a deep compassion for students that reveals itself in a helping, not punishing, attitude. After-school support programs often provide water and snacks for students, and some after-school programs include recreational activities in addition to homework help. At Riverview High School in New Brunswick,

Canada, the homework support program has a large box that contains computer discs, jump drives, calculators, pens, paper, and other supplies that some students may not be able to afford. The teachers nonchalantly tell them, "Take what you need."

Schoolwide homework support programs generally fall into one of three categories: options that find time during the school day, curricular and scheduling options, and after-school support programs.

Options That Find Time During the School Day

Lunch and homework. Assigning students to complete homework during lunch is one of the most common forms of homework support. It can be used as soon as work is late, and work can be made up in a timely manner. Lunchtime seems like a logical time to make up work, although sometimes the teacher loses lunchtime too! The downside to a lunch support program is that, no matter how it's presented, it still feels punitive to students. They miss interacting with their friends and don't feel like they've had a break. (How much less efficient are *we* later in the day when we work through lunch?) An occasional "Lunch and Work" session (Fox Middle School in Arnold, Missouri, calls it LAW) could be helpful for students, but if a student is repeatedly in LAW three or four days a week, it's not working and it's interfering with the student's needs for downtime and socializing. With 25-minute lunch periods, the amount of work that is actually accomplished may be minimal, and the sting of missing lunch with friends may create more resentment than it's worth.

Recess and homework. Equally problematic is forcing elementary students to miss recess to make up homework. Again, it seems like a logical place to find some time, albeit only a little. As with lunch programs, missing recess sometimes punishes the teacher as well, and it can hurt student learning later in the day when the student has missed the chance to get some exercise and socialize. Ken Pribish, a 3rd grade teacher, refuses to keep students in from recess to make up homework. As he sees it, "Ninety-nine percent of the time, those kids who are missing their homework are the kids who most need a break in their day. So by punishing the child, I'm punishing the learning atmosphere in my classroom. It affects my classroom management because this child needed that 15-minute break, and I just took it away from him." Again, this strategy may be effective occasionally, but when overused, students perceive it to be punitive.

Elementary classroom homework time. The easiest solution in a self-contained elementary classroom is to block out a certain amount of time daily or weekly for students to do homework in class. Faster workers may have some free time, which they could then spend in silent reading, art, peer tutoring, or helping the teacher with classroom responsibilities. Elementary teachers often assign "catch-up time" once a week for the students who need it, while other students have a choice of quiet activities.

Advisory or homeroom time. If the school has a scheduled block of nonacademic time such as an advisory or homeroom period, it can be used for students to receive teacher or peer assistance for homework. If most students are not working on schoolwork during this time, it may be better to have a few teachers assigned specifically to handle homework help. That way, students could be assigned to report to that teacher's classroom for homework help instead of to their homeroom. One teacher per grade level or subject area could serve as the homework help teacher for a month, and the duty could be rotated. Or certain teachers could volunteer to be the homework help teacher for the year and not be assigned an advisory or homeroom group. Peer tutors could also be used to assist the teachers.

Daytime homework support programs. The idea behind support offered during the school day is that making up homework is important enough to allow students to miss some regular instruction. Similar to special education pullouts in which students miss some whole-class instruction to receive one-on-one help, daytime homework support provides a location and an adult to help students complete homework assignments.

One option, though not ideal, is to use a section of the in-school suspension room as a place for students to make up homework during the school day. After all, it is a quiet place with access to a teacher for help. Obviously, it must be made clear that the purpose is not for punishment, but for the student to catch up on homework. Several options are possible. Schools may allow teachers to assign a student to the support program only during their class period, or the school may allow students to be pulled out of electives to make up academic work (although in some schools this would cause elective teachers to riot!).

One middle school administrator defended her decision this way: "Several students with one or more *F*s have been pulled from their exploratory classes in order to have a supported study period to get caught up on work. The premise is these students are in danger of being retained—we need to get their core course work to a passing level, rather than let them fail."

Boaz Middle School's "Friday Fix-It" program may require students to leave physical education, computer, library, or music classes to complete unfinished work in content areas. The teacher decides how many class periods the student needs, the teacher e-mails the homeroom teacher, and the homeroom teacher issues a ticket at the beginning of the day telling the student which class they must skip—"Skip computer class, and go to math class 2nd period" (Pyron, 2008).

Another option would be to allow students to spend entire days out of the regular classroom until work is completed. To avoid students' missing too much instruction, teachers would be expected to make accommodations and possibly excuse some work, as the student could miss new work during the time spent out of class. In this situation, it would be wise for teachers to work together to prioritize the most important assignments to be made up, to minimize the amount of time the student would be out of regular class.

The same option could be created as a separate daytime support program, which would eliminate the stigma of being in the in-school suspension room. Similar to the in-school suspension option, students could be assigned specific hours or days to catch up on work. As with in-school suspension, this program could be staffed with a full-time teacher or assigned by the hour to individual teachers or counselors. The important component is to have an adult available for help. High school students often volunteer as tutors at elementary and middle schools to get service credit for courses, clubs, or service organizations.

Curricular and Scheduling Options

Monthly late-start day. High school teachers are especially aware of how late teenagers like to stay up at night and how late they like to sleep in the morning. Some schools have instituted once-a-month late-start days, when school starts up to two hours later than normal. The intent is for students to use the extra time to complete overdue homework or work on long-term projects (Pope, 2005).

Weekly homework time. Some schools shorten each class period by a few minutes one day a week to create an hour-long block of time at the end of the school day for homework catch-up. Students stay in their last-period class or report to homeroom for the purpose of completing homework. This weekly opportunity helps to keep students from getting too far behind.

Academic Lab periods. One of the most useful ideas has been the mandatory Academic Lab period. Often used as part of an eight-block high school schedule, students must sign up for one block of Academic Lab each semester. For either 90 minutes every other day or one class period daily, Academic Lab allows students to go to other teachers for help on homework assignments, or to get that help from their Academic Lab teacher. At Parkway North High School in St. Louis, Missouri, students are assigned to the same Academic Lab teacher for all four years of high school. Special education students are assigned to a teacher in their weakest subject area. For instance, a student whose worst subject is math would be assigned to a math teacher for Academic Lab.

Study hall or independent study courses. Study halls are typically offered as noncredit electives, again giving the student a structured, quiet environment with access to a teacher. In the Dodgeland School District in Juneau, Wisconsin, study hall teachers and parents can access a Web page that lists every assignment given in every middle school class. At both the high school and the middle school, there are two shared files where the staff list their daily assignments and the names of students with any late work. The study hall teacher can access both files to see what students need to be working on.

Alternative strategies or study skills courses. Students who consistently struggle with homework may need instruction in study skills, much like what private tutoring companies offer. These are typically semester-long elective courses, and they may be taught through the communication arts department or by a special education teacher or a teacher of gifted students. In middle schools that offer 6- to 10-week exploratory courses, a 6- to 10-week study skills course may be mandated in place of another exploratory class.

Mandatory math help or credit recovery courses. In some high schools, credit recovery courses are mandatory for students who have previously failed a required course. At North Kirkwood Middle School in Kirkwood, Missouri, students who receive a *D* or an *F* in math in the 7th grade must enroll in Math Help in the 8th grade in place of an elective. This course is taken in addition to the regular 8th grade math class. Math Help is a daily elective (with a small class size) in which students receive one-on-one help with their regular 8th grade math homework.

One-hour lunch period. Some schools have decided that the best way to provide homework help is to extend the school day by extending the student lunch period from 25 minutes to 50 minutes or an hour. Students have time to eat, see their friends, and still report to homework help sessions if needed. Riverview High School in New Brunswick, Canada, and several high schools in Maryland are experimenting with the extended lunch periods. At some schools, students may be required to spend one of their two 25-minute lunch periods in tutoring, taking SAT prep, or studying.

Extended school day. A solution that seems to be growing in popularity is to extend the school day by 45 minutes or one class period. The extra time is used to coach students academically and to supervise homework. Typically, no additional homework is expected to be completed at home, with the possible exception of reading. When Sixth Street Prep School, a K–5 elementary school in Victorville, California, moved to this plan, the newspaper reported that the school had banned homework, only to say later in the story that it had done that by extending the school day to include homework time. Both teachers and parents were enthusiastic. "Gone is the stress of collecting homework and disciplining students who had nothing to turn in. In its place is extra time for the teachers to gauge if the student has grasped the concept they are teaching" (Nelson, 2007). An advantage of this plan, compared with after-school support programs, is that additional transportation is not required.

Student Teacher Access Time (STAT). STAT was created by the staff of Prairie High School in Battle Ground, Washington, to improve student learning. Other goals were to increase club and activity participation, promote school service, and improve collaboration among staff members, but STAT also allows for homework support. STAT provides a one-hour block of time each day that includes 30 minutes for lunch and 30 minutes for STAT time. STAT time may be used by students

- To get help from a teacher or peer tutor.
- To make up tests or labs.
- To spend extra time studying or completing homework.
- To attend club or activity meetings.
- To serve as a peer tutor.

The number of days each week students are required to attend STAT depends on the grades from their most recent six-week progress reports. Students with one or more *F*s must attend STAT twice a week for each class they are failing; students with no *F*s must attend two STAT sessions of their choice.

On days when students are not required to go to STAT, they have the freedom of a one-hour lunch during which they may visit the activity office, the counseling office, the library, or the career lab. Juniors and seniors without *F*s are allowed to leave campus for lunch on non-STAT days.

Each grade level is assigned a staff member as the STAT coach. The STAT coach takes attendance by scanning student ID cards and sends a weekly report to staff, encourages students to go to their teachers, and holds students accountable for their required attendance. Recently, the school improvement team added Summons Slips. Teachers may give Summons Slips to students who need extra help, also giving a copy to the STAT coach. The STAT coach can then intervene if the student fails to show up within the time frame established by the teacher and the student.

STAT provides time for struggling students to get help and rewards successful students with privileges. First implemented during the 2008–2009 school year, STAT is a work in progress. The school improvement team continues to collect data and make changes in the program to better meet the needs of students and all stakeholders.

A comprehensive daily support program. At Monticello Trails Middle School (MTMS) in Shawnee, Kansas, 45 minutes are set aside each day for the Homework Assistance Program (H.A.P.). Students are organized in interdisciplinary teams and assigned to one of their core teachers during this time. H.A.P. provides students with essential organizational skills, additional instruction, and time for homework completion. With little preparation required for its success, the Homework Assistance Program at MTMS has reinvented the traditional study hall.

Prior to H.A.P., teachers document the day's homework assignments on the E-genda, an electronic document completed by each core teacher and posted to the school Web site each day (see Figure 5.4). E-gendas are displayed during the first 15 minutes

Figure 5.4	Monticello Trails Middle School Homework E-genda

Tuesday, December 02, 2008

Monticello Trails
Homework Assistance Program (H.A.P.)

COMM. ARTS	**Objective:** TLWBAT: predict and find examples of foreshadowing. **Assignment:** Highlight Mystery Poster Rubric (not 3rd hour) **Due Date:** Wednesday, December 03, 2008
MATH	**Objective:** TLWBAT: use adjacent, vertical, supplementary, and complementary angles. **Assignment:** p. 410, 2–22 evens **Due Date:** Wednesday, December 03, 2008
SCIENCE	**Objective:** TLWBAT: identify how life is organized. **Assignment:** Read pages 4–8 in Cells text and complete the reading crossword. **Due Date:** Wednesday, December 03, 2008
SOCIAL STUDIES	**Objective:** TLWBAT: understand conflicts of Bleeding Kansas. **Assignment:** All 47 note cards for test **Due Date:** Thursday, December 04, 2008

Exploratory Classes: Students are responsible for completing on an individual basis.

TLWBAT = The Learner Will Be Able To

Source: Monticello Trails Middle School Assistance Program, Shawnee, KS. Used with permission.

of H.A.P., when students are required to copy the assignments listed into their personal agendas.

After copying the E-genda, students place their homework (complete and incomplete) on their desks and begin working on assignments due the next day. During this time, teachers check on individual students' progress by helping them identify which assignments need to be completed, as well as the priority of each. Teachers manage this component by tracking completion of assignments on a Homework Chart. According to associate principal Ben Boothe,

The E-genda has been an extremely helpful tool in our implementation of H.A.P. By displaying daily objectives, assignments, and due dates, students and parents are always aware of what is happening at school, even when an absence occurs. The E-genda is also helpful to parents who wish to monitor their child's homework on a daily basis. Communication between teachers has also increased. Teachers are now able to view each other's assignments and have become more aware of what is happening in every classroom. Because of this collaborative effort, we have seen an increase in homework completion at MTMS.

To further support students' needs and eliminate common excuses, each classroom is equipped with a copy of textbooks used in each of the core subjects as well as extra classroom supplies such as paper, pencils, calculators, and blank agenda pages. If students forget or choose not to bring the necessary supplies to complete their work, no time is lost by them leaving the room to get what they need.

Included within H.A.P. is a series of reteaching lessons. These sessions allow teachers to provide additional grade-level support and instruction to students who fail to master essential skills in the four core areas: communication arts, math, social studies, and science. H.A.P. is the ideal time to do this, since all students are available and can be flexibly grouped.

To qualify for reteaching, a student must receive less than 80 percent on a common assessment. These essential-based assessments are administered on a weekly, rotational basis. Each core subject is individually assigned a week in which to administer the common assessment during regular class time and the following week for reteaching during H.A.P. After four weeks (four core area assessments/reteaching sessions), the cycle repeats itself, allowing students to take one assessment every week in one of the four core subjects as well as receive additional support through reteaching during H.A.P.

After the administration of common assessments, teachers review the results to determine which students qualify for reteaching sessions. Once identified, these students will be regrouped during H.A.P. and required to report to that core teacher the following week.

Because small-group instruction is a key component of reteaching sessions, students originally enrolled with the core teacher providing the reteaching session are divided and temporarily redistributed to the three remaining core teachers on the team. Communication between team teachers is also necessary. After determining which students did not master the common assessment and qualify for the reteaching sessions, teachers create and distribute a list of those students to their teammates. In addition, they communicate how many days should be set aside for reteaching (usually three to four days, although the time can vary by skill). This allows the team of teachers to work together to get students where they need to be in a timely manner.

The Homework Assistance Program and reteaching sessions hold students accountable. Students quickly learn that if they fail to master essential skills, they will be required to attend reteaching sessions. This alone motivates students to work harder, increase their focus, and do their best on every assignment.

According to learning coach Dara Oswald,

> Our goal is to ensure the success of every student; failure is not an option. To make this a reality, we make it harder for students to fail than to succeed. By infusing reteaching sessions into our H.A.P. time, we provide essential support to the two kinds of students we face: those who don't get it and those who don't try. Reteaching sessions successfully provide struggling students with the additional instruction, support, and encouragement they need to succeed. By requiring students to complete each step of the reteaching process, these sessions also work to motivate reluctant learners by holding them accountable for their learning.

Teachers are also held more accountable on two levels. The first level ties into the validity of homework assignments given each day. Each assignment must be tied to a specific, student-friendly objective. These objectives drive the instruction in the building and are the foundation of every assignment given. Ben Boothe notes that "assignments are no longer given to 'fill time' but are now assigned because they are meaningful and tied to state standards." The second level of accountability relies on the teachers accepting responsibility for student learning in their classrooms. According to Dara Oswald,

> No longer does the belief that it's the teacher's job to teach and the student's to learn hold true. The staff at MTMS believes and is fully committed to the responsibility the *teacher* has to ensure that *all* students learn. Requiring teachers to reteach unmastered concepts requires them to continue teaching until every student gets it. In the past, it was easy to teach a concept once and move on. At MTMS, this is no longer an option.

After-School Homework Support Programs

After-school support programs are rapidly becoming a popular option for schools struggling with homework issues. As with other support options, they are effective only when students have been given a reasonable amount of homework and if they are implemented as soon as students are missing only a few assignments. Additional requirements for success are that students are available to stay after school, that parents allow them to stay after school, and that transportation home is provided.

Transportation is a critical component for a viable after-school support program. Logistics are simplified if transportation is already available for other after-school activities. If not, transportation becomes a huge budgetary issue. Many schools use funds from state or federal grants, such as 21st Century Grants, to subsidize transportation. If transportation is not available, some parents will volunteer to pick up their children, but often the child most in need of homework assistance does not have a parent available at that time of day.

Successful after-school support programs are both mandatory and voluntary—mandatory for students who are missing assignments, and voluntary for students who find they work better at school than at home. According to one program director, "Some students voluntarily stay for the mandatory program because they like the quiet atmosphere in which to complete their homework after school."

At Boaz Middle School, the OSCAR program (On School Campus Alternative Remediation) is offered after school three days a week for students to make up work. High school tutors come in once a week to help students identified as needing extra assistance (Pyron, 2008).

ZAP (Zeros Aren't Possible or Zeros Aren't Productive) has caught on as a popular name for after-school homework support programs. Many schools have ZAP programs, but each program may be different. Most operate similarly to the process of assigning detentions. When students fail to turn in a homework assignment, they receive a ZAP form from the teacher and are expected to report to the after-school program. Programs differ in how many missing assignments trigger a ZAP, but most programs intervene when one to three assignments are missing.

At Maplewood–Richmond Heights High School in Maplewood, Missouri, students always get a one-day grace period to turn in homework. They also have opportunities to make up work in study hall or advisory periods, and then, if necessary, are referred to the after-school homework lab. Homework labs are assigned in a timely manner after discussions between the student and the teacher. The intervention may also include an academic coach. The school's procedure is shown in Figure 5.5.

Project ASPIRE in the Dodgeland School District in Juneau, Wisconsin, is a comprehensive homework support program that serves students in grades 4 through 12. Started in 2004, it has succeeded in reducing the failure rate at all grade levels. Project

Figure 5.5	Homework Lab Procedures at Maplewood–Richmond Heights High School		
Path A	**Path B**	**Path C**
• Student fails to complete assignment on time. Teacher assigns student a homework ticket to attend Homework Lab. • Assignment is completed in study hall or advisory. Study hall/advisory teacher signs the homework ticket. Student does not need to attend Homework Lab.	• Student fails to complete assignment on time. Teacher assigns student a homework ticket to attend Homework Lab. • Student attends Homework Lab and completes assignment. Homework Lab teacher signs homework ticket.	• Student fails to complete assignment on time. Teacher assigns student a homework ticket to attend Homework Lab. • Student fails to attend Homework Lab. Assignment is incomplete. • Student is removed from study hall, advisory, or lunch period. Student meets with academic coach for homework assistance. Academic coach signs student's homework ticket. • Extracurricular activities could be withheld until the student makes up the lab. Student might not be allowed to participate (play or be a spectator) in any activity the school holds. This includes sports and clubs. Saturday detention may also be assigned.

Source: Maplewood–Richmond Heights High School, Maplewood, MO. Used with permission.

ASPIRE is funded by a grant for Alternative Education Programs from the state of Wisconsin. A letter is sent home to parents at the beginning of the year explaining the purpose of the program and that after-school transportation is provided. The basics of the program are shown in Figure 5.6, but the true effect is better understood by reading a letter from the project's coordinator, Annette Thompson:

> We continue to "fight the good fight" with both the voluntary after-school homework programs (PALS in the elementary and Homework Help at the middle school/high school level), as well as the mandatory Extended Day program for students referred for not completing their work.
>
> Homework Help and PALS meet Tuesday and Thursday for one hour, and then the students have an hour of supervised recreational activity. This is done in partnership with our federal PEP grant and the local recreation department. We provide water bottles and healthy snacks for these voluntary programs. This has increased our participation in the after-school homework programs and helps meet not only the academic needs of our students, but also their physical and emotional needs.
>
> New at the high school level this year are two "shared files" where the staff list their assignments as well as any missing work on our server. Study hall personnel check the site, which diminishes some of the "I don't have anything to do" syndrome. The middle school has had a similar system for the last three years. The only issue with these systems is the frequency and accuracy of the updates.
>
> A positive addition to our voluntary homework program is that both the National Honor Society and the high school health class require community service hours. We have a number of high school students volunteering their time for these after-school programs, building great relationships and modeling positive attitudes toward school.
>
> By no means have we solved the homework issue at our schools, but at least we are being proactive in sending the message to the students and community that schoolwork is

Figure 5.6	Project ASPIRE, Dodgeland School District

Middle School Turn Around Program (TAP)

- Supportive study hall
- Full-time teacher
- Late work site is maintained in a shared folder
- Daily listing of assigned homework is accessible electronically
- Teacher communicates with parents about homework
- Approximately 12 percent of middle school students participate
- Voluntary

High School Turn Around Program (TAP)

- 42-minute supportive study hall/student resource center
- Full-time teacher
- Approximately 8 percent of high school students participate
- Voluntary

PALS

- 4th and 5th graders
- Twice a week after school, followed by supervised recreational activities
- Approximately 22 percent of students participate
- Enrollment based on teacher referral and subsequent parent permission

Homework Help

- After-school support for 6th, 7th, and 8th graders
- Snacks, recreation, and tutoring
- Voluntary—students drop in as needed
- Teachers from core subjects are available during this time

Aspire to Improve Study Sessions

- After-school support for high school students
- Voluntary
- Supported by teachers in core subject areas

(continued)

Figure 5.6	Project ASPIRE, Dodgeland School District (Continued)

Extended Day

- 4th–8th graders and 9th–12th graders
- Mandatory for students missing 3 or more assignments
- Monday through Thursday, 3–5 p.m.
- Transportation provided

Remedial Course for 10th–12th Graders

- For students who failed one or more classes OR
- Are two or more years below age group in basic skills

GED Option 2

- School within a school
- 12th graders 17 years old and older
- Meets in late afternoon to allow students access to employment
- Modified school day
- Successful students earn a regular high school diploma

Source: From Dodgeland School District, Juneau, WI. Used with permission.

important, and the expectation is that what is assigned will be completed in a timely and acceptable manner. For the most part, the students are heeding this message. We are learning that all of these components need to be in place. If there is a break in this continuum of interventions, then the successful outcomes are diminished.

—Annette

Summing Up

The new homework paradigm outlined in this book offers a comprehensive plan for homework reform. But comprehensive reform requires a long-term commitment from teachers, administrators, and parents, and a climate that is open to change. Depending on the unique needs of individual communities, that change may happen quickly or may need to move more slowly. For schools that need time to soften ingrained attitudes, minor changes can be helpful in beginning the process. For those schools, the following "baby steps" may be a good place to start:

- Limit the percentage that homework may count in the grade.
- Revise late policies.
- Limit the number of subjects in which homework is assigned each night.
- Limit the weight of the backpack.
- Set weekly or nightly time limits.
- Prohibit weekend or holiday homework.
- Coordinate homework with a calendar limiting the number of tests or projects at a given time.
- Limit the number of AP classes that students may take in one semester.

Homework reform is a worthwhile endeavor that has the potential to enhance student learning, reduce failure, improve student motivation, and strengthen the parent-teacher relationship. The key to success is raising awareness, letting go of some traditional attitudes and practices, and putting the well-being of children first.

• • •

Afterword

Homework is a unique educational practice. Of all the learning strategies a teacher may use, it is the only one that crosses the boundary separating school and home, encompassing the two worlds of school and home that all children inhabit. Given the complexity of family life and the diversity of students today, it is no surprise that the practice of homework is challenging—and in some communities, controversial.

The scope of our challenges reflects the wide social and economic diversity of our schools. Our challenges range from reeling in the extreme homework overload (wrongly equated with rigor) that is often prevalent in highly competitive schools, to helping teachers in impoverished schools who struggle to get students to complete even the simplest of homework tasks. Our frustrations are compounded by the nagging feeling that, if we could just get it right, homework could be a real asset to learning. Our instincts are not wrong.

At its best, homework in reasonable amounts can support and enhance learning, provide feedback to teachers about learning, allow students to practice skills and deepen their knowledge, and instill confidence within students when they successfully complete tasks on their own.

But at its worst, homework may widen the achievement gap and may unfairly discriminate against students who are unable to work at home. At its worst, homework may dampen student enthusiasm and love of learning and may lead to frustration and feelings of incompetence. When homework is excessive, it may compromise the healthy balance between work, play, and downtime that all children need.

To improve homework practices, we must do the following:

• First, acknowledge our inborn attitudes about homework and question the folklore behind homework traditions.

• Examine homework research with a critical eye and trust what our experience with learners has taught us.

• Accept not only that parenting and families have changed, but also that the relationship between parents and schools has changed. We must respect the right of parents to control their child's free time, and we must work cooperatively with parents to determine homework guidelines.

To implement homework effectively, we must do the following:

• Connect homework to classroom learning and clearly identify the purpose of each assignment.

• Provide students with relevant tasks that they can complete without adult help.

• Use what we know about learning to design homework appropriate for individual students.

• Facilitate two-way communication between teachers and students and between teachers and parents.

• Respect the role of motivation and winning streaks in the decisions that students make to tackle and persist with homework tasks.

To implement homework equitably, we must do the following:

• Assign reasonable amounts of homework.
• Differentiate homework for individual needs.
• Be sensitive about the limitations of home environments.
• Accept that not all students can or will work at home.

- Remove failure as an option by minimizing or eliminating the grading of homework.
- Establish school-sponsored homework support programs.

Homework reform can be a wonderful catalyst for total school reform. An examination of homework practices may jump-start conversations about curriculum standards, grading practices, and teaching strategies. Reform of homework practices may drive future reform of assessment, curriculum, and instructional practices.

But the journey of homework reform is not a simple one. Along the way there will be resistance, roadblocks to change, and a wide diversity of opinions. Parents, teachers, or administrators may cling to outdated beliefs, or they may be mired in the inertia of old habits. Consensus may be difficult as we struggle to find that common ground where school and family values intersect. But within the context of the needs of individual communities and the reality of family's everyday lives, consensus can be found.

You are not alone in your quest for change—thousands of schools around the world have changed their homework practices, and many more have begun the process of reform. So stay the course and keep the faith. You are undoing 100 years of traditional attitudes and beliefs to provide more meaningful learning experiences for your students. It is valuable and important work.

Homework Survey for Parents

The purpose of this survey is to learn more about homework practices in your school and to find out your opinions about homework. Teachers and students will also be asked to complete surveys. All surveys are anonymous.

Basic information

Grade level of child _____

Sex of child _____

Does your child receive special education services?
(Circle one.)   Yes   No   I don't know

Does your child participate in the gifted program?
(Circle one.)   Yes   No   I don't know

Time spent on homework

1. On average, how much time does your child spend on homework on weekday evenings?

2. On average, how much time does your child spend on homework on weekends?

3. What do you feel is an appropriate amount of homework for your child's grade level?

4. How do you feel about weekend homework and homework over holiday vacations?

5. How much control should parents have over the amount of homework their child has? (Check all that apply to your child.)

___ I should be able to request a limit on the amount of homework.

___ I should be able to request additional homework for my child.

___ I should be able to excuse my child from homework when I feel it is necessary.

Other _____

Purpose or value of homework

6. How often do you understand the value of the homework assignment to your child's learning?

7. How often does the homework appear to be busywork?

Difficulty of homework/child's work habits

8. Can your child complete homework without your help or supervision?

___ Yes, but doesn't want to

___ Yes, usually

___ Yes, always

___ Not usually

___ Never

Other _____

9. Does your child have special needs or special circumstances that influence the ability to complete homework? (Check all that apply to your child.)

___ My child takes medication for school that has worn off before homework is done.

___ My child needs a lot of downtime to relax after a hard day at school.

___ My child has many responsibilities at home that leave little time for homework.

___ My child is involved in many outside activities that leave little time for homework.

___ My child spends little time at home on weekdays because of extended day care, babysitters, or visitation with noncustodial parents.

Other _____

10. If your child has difficulty working alone, to what do you attribute the problem? (Check all that apply to your child.)

___ My child is easily frustrated.

___ There are too many distractions.

___ My child is tired/unable to focus.

___ My child resents having to work at home.

___ Homework directions are not clear.

___ The assignment is too hard.

Other_____

11. Does your child have organizational problems related to homework? (Check all that apply to your child.)

___ My child doesn't realize there is a homework assignment.

___ My child forgets to write the assignment down.

___ My child forgets to bring home books or materials.

___ My child completes homework but forgets to turn it in or loses track of it.

Other_____

12. What resources do you have at home to assist your child in doing homework? (Check all that apply.)

___ A quiet place to work

___ Dictionary

___ Encyclopedia

___ Internet access

___ An adult with time to help

13. How involved are you in your child's homework? (Check **all** statements that apply to you.)

___ I don't get involved in my child's homework.

___ I check to see that my child's homework is done.

___ I have corrected my child's mistakes on homework.

___ I have completed homework for my child just to get it done.

___ I sometimes have trouble helping my child because I don't understand the directions.

___ I sometimes have trouble helping my child because I don't understand the material.

___ I'm not sure *how much* I should help my child with homework.

___ I have occasionally prohibited my child from doing homework because it interfered with sleep or family time.

Other_____

14. What could teachers do to make the homework process better and less stressful for your child? (Check all that you agree with.)

___ Stop giving homework altogether.

___ Give less homework.

___ Make homework optional or for extra credit.

___ Make sure my child has written down the homework assignment.

___ Make sure the child understands the homework.

___ Provide a copy of the textbook to keep at home.

___ Give clearer instructions to students about homework.

___ Set a maximum amount of time the child should work on each assignment.

___ Prioritize assignments in case the child does not have time to complete all homework.

___ Give assignments further in advance of the due date.

___ Give students more than one day to complete assignments.

___ Make assignments accessible from home by the use of a homework phone line or Web site.

___ Allow parents to call the teacher at home when necessary.

___ Let parents know how homework is graded and what percentage of the total quarter grade it accounts for.

___ Give parents guidance on *how* to help with homework and *how much* to help.

___ Provide a cover sheet that encourages parents to communicate about homework in writing to the teacher.

References

Allington, R. L. (2002, November). You can't learn much from books you can't read. *Educational Leadership, 60*(3), 16–19.

Allington, R. L. (2005). Ideology is still trumping evidence. *Phi Delta Kappan, 86*(6), 462.

Andrade, H. (2007, December–2008, January). Self-assessment through rubrics. *Educational Leadership, 65*(4), 60–63.

Baker, D. P., & LeTendre, G. K. (2005). *National differences, global similarities: World culture and the future of schooling.* Stanford, CA: Stanford University Press.

Begley, S. (1998, March 30). Homework doesn't help. *Newsweek,* 50–51.

Bempechat, J. (2004). The motivational benefits of homework: A social-cognitive perspective. *Theory into Practice, 43*(3), 189–196.

Bennett, S., & Kalish, N. (2006). *The case against homework: How homework is hurting our children and what we can do about it.* New York: Crown Publishers.

Brookhart, S. M. (2007, December–2008, January). Feedback that fits. *Educational Leadership, 65*(4), 54–59.

Bryan, T., & Burstein, K. (2004). Improving homework completion and academic performance: Lessons from special education. *Theory into Practice, 43*(3), 213–219.

Buell, J. (2004). *Closing the book on homework: Enhancing public education and freeing family time.* Philadelphia: Temple University Press.

Christopher, S. (2007, December–2008, January). Homework: A few practice arrows. *Educational Leadership, 65*(4), 74–75.

Connors, N. A. (1992). *Homework: A new direction.* Columbus, OH: Corwin Press.

Cool, V., & Keith, T. Z. (1991). Testing a model of school learning: Direct and indirect effects on academic achievement. *Contemporary Educational Psychology, 16,* 28–44.

Cooper, H. (1989a). *Homework.* White Plains, NY: Longman.

Cooper, H. (1989b, November). Synthesis of research on homework. *Educational Leadership, 47*(3), 85–91.

Cooper, H. (1994). *The battle over homework: An administrator's guide to setting sound and effective policies.* Thousand Oaks, CA: Corwin Press.

Cooper, H. (2001). *The battle over homework: Common ground for administrators, teachers, and parents* (2nd ed.). Thousand Oaks, CA: Corwin Press.

Cooper, H. (2007). *The battle over homework: Common ground for administrators, teachers, and parents* (3rd ed.). Thousand Oaks, CA: Corwin Press.

Cooper, H., Lindsay, J. L., Nye, B., & Greathouse, S. (1998). Relationships among attitudes about homework, amount of homework assigned and completed, and student achievement. *Journal of Educational Psychology, 90*(1), 70–83.

Cooper, H., Robinson, J. C., & Patall, E. A. (2006). Does homework improve academic achievement? A synthesis of research, 1987–2003. *Review of Educational Research, 76*(1), 1–62.

Cooper, H., & Valentine, J. C. (2001). Using research to answer practical questions about homework. *Educational Psychologist, 36*(3), 143–153.

Corno, L. (1996). Homework is a complicated thing. *Educational Researcher, 25*(8), 27–30.

Corno, L., & Xu, J. (2004). Homework as the job of childhood. *Theory into Practice, 43*(3), 227–233.

Costa, A., & Kallick, B. (2004, September). Launching self-directed learners. *Educational Leadership, 62*(1), 51–55.

Crain, W. (2003). *Reclaiming childhood: Letting children be children in our achievement-oriented society.* New York: Holt.

Darling-Hammond, L., & Ifill-Lynch, O. (2006, February). If they'd only do their work! *Educational Leadership, 63*(5), 8–13.

Dunn, R. (2003). *Research on the Dunn and Dunn model of learning styles.* Jamaica, NY: St. John's University.

Dunn, R., & Dunn, K. (1978). *Teaching students through their individual learning styles.* Reston, VA: Reston Publications.

Eisner, E. (2002). The kind of schools we need. *Phi Delta Kappan, 83*(8), 576–583.

Eisner, E. W. (2003, December–2004, January). Preparing for today and tomorrow. *Educational Leadership, 61*(4), 6–11.

Elkind, D. (1981). *The hurried child: Growing up too fast too soon.* Reading, MA: Addison-Wesley.

Epstein, J. L., & Van Voorhis, F. L. (2001). More than minutes: Teachers' roles in designing homework. *Educational Psychologist, 36*(3), 181–193.

Fisher, D., & Frey, N. (2007). *Checking for understanding: Formative assessment techniques for your classroom.* Alexandria, VA: ASCD.

Frieman, B. B. (2001). *What teachers need to know about children at risk.* Boston: McGraw-Hill.

Galley, M. (2001, February 21). Lugging heavy backpacks hurts children, study says. *Education Week,* 5.

Gardner, H. (1999). *Intelligence reframed: Multiple intelligences for the 21st century.* New York: Simon and Schuster.

Garner, B. K. (2008). When students seem stalled. *Educational Leadership, 65*(6), 32–38.

Gebhard, M. (2002, December–2003, January). Getting past "See spot run." *Educational Leadership, 60*(4), 35–39.

Gill, B., & Schlossman, S. (1996). A sin against childhood: Progressive education and the crusade to abolish homework, 1897–1941. *American Journal of Education, 105*(1), 27–66.

Gill, B., & Schlossman, S. (2000). The lost cause of homework reform. *American Journal of Education, 109*(1), 27–36.

Gill, B. P., & Schlossman, S. L. (2004). Villain or savior? The American discourse on homework, 1850–2003. *Theory into Practice, 43*(3), 174–181.

Ginsburg, K. R. (2007). The importance of play in promoting healthy child development and maintaining strong parent-child bonds. *Pediatrics, 119*(1), 182–191.

Glasser, W. (1992). *The quality school: Managing students without coercion.* New York: HarperCollins.

Goldberg, K. (2007, April). *The homework trap.* Paper presented at the annual meeting of the American Educational Research Association, Chicago.

Guskey, T. R. (2003, October). How classroom assessments improve learning. *Educational Leadership, 52*(2), 14–20.

Guskey, T. R., & Anderman, E. M. (2008). Students at bat. *Educational Leadership, 66*(3), 8–14.

Guskey, T. R., & Bailey, J. M. (2001). *Developing grading and reporting systems for student learning.* Thousand Oaks, CA: Corwin Press.

Hart, B., & Risley, T. R. (1995). *Meaningful differences in the everyday experience of young American children.* Baltimore: P. H. Brookes.

Honore, C. (2004). *In praise of slowness: Challenging the cult of speed.* New York: HarperCollins.

Huguelet, J. (2007, May). No more haves and have-nots. *Educational Leadership, 64*(8), 45–47.

Intrator, S. M. (2004, September). The engaged classroom. *Educational Leadership, 62*(1), 20–24.

Jackson, R. R. (2009). *Never work harder than your students and other principles of great teaching.* Alexandria, VA: ASCD.

Jensen, E. (2000). *Brain-based learning.* San Diego, CA: The Brain Store.

Jones, R. (2001). How parents can support learning. *American School Board Journal, 188*(9), 18–22.

Kantrowitz, B., & Tyre, P. (2006, May 22). The fine art of letting go. *Newsweek,* 49–58.

Keefe, J. W., & Jenkins, J. M. (2002). Personalized instruction. *Phi Delta Kappan, 83*(6), 440–448.

Keith, T. Z. (1982). Time spent on homework and high school grades: A large-sample path analysis. *Journal of Educational Psychology, 74*(2), 248–253.

Keith, T. Z., & Cool, V. A. (1992). Testing models of school learning: Effects of quality instruction, motivation, academic coursework, and homework on academic achievement. *School Psychology Quarterly, 7*(3), 207–226.

Kohn, A. (1998). *What to look for in classrooms . . . and other essays.* San Francisco: Jossey-Bass.

Kohn, A. (1999). *Punished by rewards: The trouble with gold stars, incentive plans, A's, praise, and other bribes* (2nd ed.). New York: Houghton Mifflin.

Kohn, A. (2000). *The case against standardized testing: Raising the scores, ruining the schools.* Portsmouth, NH: Heinemann.

Kohn, A. (2006). *The homework myth: Why our kids get too much of a bad thing.* Cambridge, MA: Da Capo Press.

Kralovec, E., & Buell, J. (2000). *The end of homework: How homework disrupts families, overburdens children, and limits learning.* Boston: Beacon Press.

Levine, M., M.D. (2003). *The myth of laziness.* New York: Simon and Schuster.

Louv, R. (2005). *Last child in the woods: Saving our children from nature deficit disorder.* Chapel Hill, NC: Algonquin Books of Chapel Hill.

Margolis, H. (2005). Resolving struggling learners' homework difficulties: Working with elementary school learners and parents. *Preventing School Failure, 50*(1), 5–12.

Marzano, R. J., & Pickering, D. J. (2007, March). The case for and against homework. *Educational Leadership, 64*(6), 74–79.

Marzano, R. J., Pickering, D. J., & Pollock, J. E. (2001). *Classroom instruction that works: Research-based strategies for increasing student achievement.* Alexandria, VA: ASCD.

Minotti, J. L. (2005). Effects of learning-style-based homework prescriptions on the achievement and attitudes of middle school students. *NASSP Bulletin, 89*(642), 67–89.

Moore, M. J., White, G. L., & Moore, D. L. (2007). Association of relative backpack weight with reported pain site, medical utilization, and lost school time in children and adolescents. *The Journal of School Health, 77*(5), 232–239.

National Commission on Excellence in Education. (1983). *A nation at risk: The imperative for educational reform.* Washington, DC: Author.

Nelson, J. (2007, July 20). Ban homework. *San Francisco Chronicle,* p. B11.

O'Connor, K. (2002). *How to grade for learning: Linking grades to standards.* Thousand Oaks, CA: Corwin Press.

O'Connor, K. (2007). *A repair kit for grading: 15 fixes for broken grades.* Portland, OR: Educational Testing Service.

Olson, K. (2008). The wounded student. *Educational Leadership, 65*(6), 46–49.

Oyola, M. (2006, November 18). Vacations from school: Pencil in some time off. *St. Louis Post-Dispatch,* pp. A1, A23.

Past, R. J. (2006). Homework that helps. *Principal Leadership, 7*(1), 8–9.

Patterson, W. (2003). Breaking out of our boxes. *Phi Delta Kappan, 84*(8), 569–574.

Payne, R. (2001). *A framework for understanding poverty.* Highlands, TX: aha! Process, Inc.

Payne, R. (2008). Nine powerful practices. *Educational Leadership, 65*(7), 48–52.

Pellegrini, A. D. (2005). *Recess: Its role in education and development.* Mahwah, NJ: Erlbaum Associates.

Perkins-Gough, D. (2006, February). Accelerating the learning of low achievers. *Educational Leadership, 63*(5), 88–90.

Pethokoukis, J. M. (2006, June 26). Anxiety attack. *U.S. News & World Report,* pp. 42–45.

Pope, D. C. (2001). *"Doing school": How we are creating a generation of stressed out, materialistic, and miseducated students.* New Haven, CT: Yale University Press.

Pope, D. C. (2005, April). Help for stressed students. *Educational Leadership, 62*(7), 33–37.

Popham, W. J. (2008). *Transformative assessment.* Alexandria, VA: ASCD.

Postman, N., & Weingartner, C. (1969). *Teaching as a subversive activity.* New York: Delacorte Press.

Pyron, J. (2008). The road from good to great. *Working Toward Excellence, 8*(1), 7–11.

Raebeck, B. (1992). *Transforming middle schools: A guide to whole-school change.* Lancaster, PA: Technomic.

Ratnesar, R. (1999, January 25). The homework ate my family. *Time,* 55–63.

Rothstein, R. (2004). *Class and schools: Using social, economic, and educational reform to close the black-white achievement gap.* New York: Teachers College Press.

Sagor, R. (2002, September). Lessons from skateboarders. *Educational Leadership, 60*(1), 34–38.

Sagor, R. (2008). Cultivating optimism in the classroom. *Educational Leadership, 65*(6), 26–31.

Stiggins, R. J. (2005). *Student-involved assessment for learning.* Upper Saddle River, NJ: Pearson.

Stiggins, R. (2007, May). Assessment through the student's eyes. *Educational Leadership, 64*(8), 22–26.

Taffel, R. (2001). *The second family.* New York: St. Martin's Press.

Taylor, J. (2007). *Motivating the uncooperative student: Redeeming discouragement and attitude problems.* Monmouth, OR: ADD Plus.

Tell, C. (2000). Generation what? Connecting with today's youth. *Educational Leadership, 57*(4), 8–13.

Thornburgh, N. (2006, April 9). Dropout nation. *Time,* 30–40.

Tomlinson, C. (1999). *The differentiated classroom: Responding to the needs of all learners.* Alexandria, VA: ASCD.

Tomlinson, C. (2003, October). Deciding to teach them all. *Educational Leadership, 61*(2), 7–11.

Tomlinson, C. A., & McTighe, J. (2006). *Integrating differentiated instruction and Understanding by Design: Connecting content and kids.* Alexandria, VA: ASCD.

Trautwein, U., & Koller, O. (2003). The relationship between homework and achievement—still much of a mystery. *Educational Psychology Review, 15*(2), 115–145.

Trautwein, U., Koller, O., Schmitz, B., & Baumert, J. (2002). Do homework assignments enhance achievement? A multilevel analysis in 7th grade mathematics. *Contemporary Educational Psychology, 27,* 26–50.

Tyre, P. (2006, September 11). The new first grade: Too much, too soon? *Newsweek,* 34–44.

Vatterott, C. (2003, January). There's something wrong with homework. *Principal,* 64.

Vatterott, C. (2005, October/November). Mom and Dad aren't taking algebra this year. *Our Children,* 4–7.

Vatterott, C. (2007). *Becoming a middle level teacher: Student-focused teaching of early adolescents.* New York: McGraw-Hill.

Wharton, P. M. (2001). The forgotten voices of homework: Views of students. *Educational Psychologist, 36*(3), 155–165.

Wheelock, A., & Dorman, G. (1988). *Before it's too late: Dropout prevention in the middle grades.* Carrboro, NC: Center for Early Adolescence.

Wildman, P. R. (1968). Homework pressures. *Peabody Journal of Education, 45*(4), 204.

Williamson, R., & Johnston, J. H. (1999). Challenging orthodoxy: An emerging agenda for middle level reform. *Middle School Journal, 30*(4), 10–17.

Wormeli, R. (2003). *Day one and beyond: Practical matters for new middle level teachers.* Columbus, OH: National Middle School Association.

Wright, J. (2006). Learning interventions for struggling students. *Education Digest, 71*(5), 35–39.

Zuckerman, M. B. (2006, June 4). Rich man, poor man. *U.S. News & World Report,* pp. 71–72.

Index

• • •

About the Author

Dr. Cathy Vatterott is an associate professor of education at the University of Missouri–St. Louis, where she trains preservice middle school teachers. She is a former middle school and high school teacher and middle school principal. She is the author of numerous articles about education, including "Homework Myths" and "There's Something Wrong with Homework," and two books, *Academic Success Through Empowering Students* (National Middle School Association, 1999) and *Becoming a Middle Level Teacher: Student-Focused Teaching of Early Adolescents* (McGraw-Hill, 2007).

She first became interested in homework as the frustrated parent of a 5th grader with learning disabilities. Since then, she has presented her homework research to more than 6,000 educators and parents in the United States, Canada, and Europe. She has conducted professional development institutes about homework for ASCD since 2004. She has been interviewed as a homework expert for articles appearing in such publications as *Parents* magazine, *Better Homes and Gardens* magazine, *Child* magazine, *Working*

Mother magazine, the *Globe and Mail* (Canada's national newspaper), and numerous U.S. newspapers and educational Web sites, as well as for radio and television programs. Some of her presentation materials and unpublished writings about homework can be found at her Web site, www.homeworklady.com. She can be reached through her Web site or at Vatterott@umsl.edu.